EDUCATIONAL COUNTER-CULTURES
CONFRONTATIONS, IMAGES, VISION

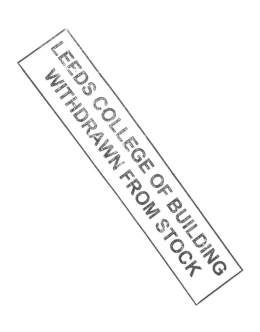
Discourse Power Resistance Volume 3

Educational Counter-Cultures

CONFRONTATIONS, IMAGES, VISION

edited by Jerome Satterthwaite,
Elizabeth Atkinson and Wendy Martin

Trentham Books
Stoke on Trent, UK and Sterling, USA

Trentham Books Limited

Westview House	22883 Quicksilver Drive
734 London Road	Sterling
Oakhill	VA 20166-2012
Stoke on Trent	USA
Staffordshire	
England ST4 5NP	

First published 2004

British Library Cataloguing-in-Publication Data
A catalogue record for this book is available from the British Library

1 85856 338 0

Designed and typeset by Trentham Print Design Ltd., Chester and printed in Great Britain by Cromwell Press Ltd, Wiltshire.

Contents

Discourse Power Resistance Series

SERIES EDITORS:
JEROME SATTERTHWAITE AND ELIZABETH ATKINSON

In the Spring of 2002, the first international Discourse Power Resistance conference was held in Plymouth, UK, to examine pressing issues in contemporary education. Key debates from this conference were brought together in our first book, *Discourse, Power, Resistance: challenging the rhetoric of contemporary education*, published in the Spring of 2003. The second conference on this theme, already fondly known as 'DPR', had given rise to two further books, presenting powerful analyses of global moves in education and offering rich and varied forms of resistance to them. Together, these three books form the opening titles in the new *Discourse, Power, Resistance* book series, published by Trentham. This series, which is intended for students, teachers, trainers, lecturers, researchers and those responsible for shaping educational policy, aims to promote a radical re-thinking of educational theory and practice, to offer a sustained and thoughtful challenge to the *status quo* in education and to put forward positive and exciting alternatives.

Other titles in the series

Discourse, Power, Resistance: Challenging the Rhetoric of Contemporary Education (2003) edited by Jerome Satterthwaite and Elizabeth Atkinson and Ken Gale

The Disciplining of Education: New Languages of Power and Resistance (2004) edited by Jerome Satterthwaite, Elizabeth Atkinson and Wendy Martin

Introduction

ELIZABETH ATKINSON

This book is a song of resistance. Drawing on rich cross-cultural perspectives from around the world, the authors challenge readers to envision new ways of thinking for education: ways which draw on the arts, on imagination and on the collective experience of subjugated cultures and ways of knowing.

Part One, *Collisions, Collusions*, focuses on the impact of current educational policy in the US and the UK within the context of globalised educational discourses. Michael W. Apple opens with a critique of the 'new hegemonic blocks' in US education policy, in which he deconstructs the political and rhetorical moves by which the notion of educating the 'right' way is maintained. Mike Cole and Terry Wrigley examine and rethink what they see as discourses of despair embedded in the opposing paradigms of postmodernism and the School Effectiveness and School Improvement movements, and offer their own counter-discourses of resistance and hope.

Part Two, *Cultural Conflict*, brings together diverse and often opposing voices with a common interest in real lives: the common theme here is the subjugation of marginalised voices, and their resistance in the face of discourses of power. Elizabeth Atkinson and Richard Bond explore two forms of silencing: the silencing of sexualities within educational research and practice and that of indigenous voices within Canadian Higher Education. Farid Panjwani and Halleli Pinson analyse the contested discourses of power and control within religious education in Pakistan and citizenship education in Israel. Finally, Jean McNiff argues, on the basis of her work in Northern Ireland, Palestine, Israel and South Africa, for a reconceptualisation of peace education based on a real recognition of the agonistic nature of human relations.

Part Three, *Images, Vision*, invites us to turn from what we think we know to what we do not know, as a form of resistance to the forces which drive us away from our deeper instincts. Jerome Satterthwaite brings the unknowing of fourteenth century mysticism together with that of contemporary astrophysics to explore what it is that can be discovered beyond the rational bounds of prescriptive teaching and assessment. Alan Bleakley analyses ways of knowing in the field of medicine which are aesthetic and interpretive rather than logical and rational. Finally, John Danvers and Victoria Perselli challenge our certainties and assumptions by disrupting the logic of language and representation and evoking the symbolic power of images as sites of multiple signification. Discourses of power and resistance have played a particular part in shaping this final section of the book: the debate between authors and editors over the extent to which readers should be left to make their own interpretations has added a further dimension to the issues under discussion, and revealed the force of the current drive for transparency in educational writing and practice.

This book is for all those, whether students, tutors or researchers, who are interested in opposing dominant educational discourses across the world through the exploration of other ways of knowing. Together, these authors offer multiple perspectives on resistance with a common purpose: to see, think and do education otherwise.

PART ONE
COLLISIONS, COLLUSIONS

1

Doing things the 'Right' way: legitimating educational inequalities in conservative times

MICHAEL W. APPLE

Michael Apple writes with formidable political insight about the tightening grip on education in the United States of the combination of four powerful groups. He argues that Neo-Liberals, Neo-Conservatives, the Christian Right and the Professional Middle Class have increasingly dominated the educational agenda, prescribing and pro- scribing so as to bring about a new and frightening rightist turn in policy and practice. This chapter sets the tone for the sustained critique of educational conservatism which is developed in this section by Cole and Wrigley.

Introduction

Education is a site of struggle and compromise. It also serves as a proxy, for larger battles over what our institutions should do, who they should serve, and who should make these decisions. Education is one of the major arenas in which resources, power, and ideology specific to policy, finance, curriculum, pedagogy, and evaluation are worked through. Thus, education is both cause and effect, deter- mining and determined. Because of this, no one chapter could hope to give a complete picture of this complexity. What I hope to do instead is to provide an outline of some of the major tensions surrounding education in the United States as it moves in conservative directions.

A key word here is directions. The plural is crucial to my arguments, since as I document in more detail elsewhere[1] there are multiple and at times contradictory tendencies within the rightist turn.

The rightward turn has been the result of the successful struggle by the right to form a broad-based alliance. This new alliance has been successful in part because it has been able to win the battle over common sense. That is, it has creatively stitched together different social tendencies and commitments and has organised them under its own general leadership in issues dealing with social welfare, culture, the economy, and, as we shall see in this chapter, education. Its aim in educational and social policy is what I have called 'conservative modernisation.'[2] There are four major elements within this alliance. Each has its own relatively autonomous history and dynamics but each has also been sutured into the more general conservative movement. These elements include neo-liberals, neo-conservatives, authoritarian populists, and a particular fraction of the upwardly mobile professional and managerial new middle class. I shall pay particular attention to the first two of these groups here since they – and especially neo-liberals – are currently in leadership in this alliance to reform education.

Neo-Liberalism: Schooling, Choice and Democracy

Neo-liberals are the most powerful element within the alliance supporting conservative modernisation. They are guided by a vision of the weak state. Thus, what is private is necessarily good and what is public is necessarily bad. Public institutions such as schools are seen as 'black holes' into which money is poured – and then seemingly disappears – but which do not provide anywhere near adequate results. For neo-liberals, there is one form of rationality that is more powerful than any other – economic rationality. Efficiency and an ethic of cost-benefit analysis are the dominant norms. All people are to act in ways that maximise their own personal benefits. Indeed, behind this position is an empirical claim that this is how *all* rational actors act. Yet, rather than being a neutral description of the world of social motivation, this is actually a construction of the world around the valuative characteristics of an efficiently acquisitive class type.

Underpinning this position is a vision of students as human capital. The world is intensely competitive economically, and students – as

4

future workers – must be given the requisite skills and dispositions to compete efficiently and effectively. Further, any money spent on schools that is not directly related to these economic goals is suspect. In fact, as 'black holes,' schools and other public services, as they are currently organised and controlled, waste economic resources that should go into private enterprise. Thus, not only are public schools failing our children as future workers, but like nearly all public institutions they are sucking the financial life out of this society. Partly this is the result of 'producer capture.' Schools are built for teachers and state bureaucrats, not consumers. They respond to the demands of professionals and other selfish state workers, not the consumers who rely on them.

The idea of the 'consumer' is crucial here. For neo-liberals, the world in essence is a vast supermarket. Consumer choice is the guarantor of democracy. In effect, education is seen as simply one more product like bread, cars, and television.[3] By turning it over to the market through voucher and choice plans, it will be largely self-regulating. Thus, democracy is turned into consumption practices. In these plans, the ideal of the citizen is that of the purchaser. The ideological effects of this are momentous. Rather than democracy being a *political* concept, it is transformed into a wholly *economic* concept. The message of such policies is what might best be called 'arithmetical particularism,' in which the unattached individual – as a consumer – is deraced, declassed, and degendered.[4]

With their emphasis on the consumer rather than the producer, neo-liberal policies need also to be seen as part of a more extensive attack on government employees. In education in particular, they constitute an offensive against teacher unions who are seen to be much too powerful and much too costly. While perhaps not conscious, this needs to be interpreted as part of a longer history of attacks on women's labour, since the vast majority of teachers in the United States – as in so many other nations – are women.[5]

Varied policy initiatives have emerged from the neo-liberal segments of the new hegemonic alliance. Most have centered around either creating closer linkages between education and the economy or placing schools themselves into the market. The former is represented by widespread proposals for 'school to work' and 'education for employment' programmes, and by vigorous cost-cutting attacks on the 'bloated state.' The latter is no less widespread and is becoming increasingly powerful. It is represented by both national and state-by-state proposals for voucher and choice programs.[6] These include providing public money for private and religious schools (although these are highly contested proposals). Behind this is a plan to subject schools to the discipline of market competition. Such quasi-market solutions are among the most divisive and hotly debated policy issues in the entire nation, with important court cases concerning funding for private and/or religious schools through voucher mechanisms having been decided or now being closely watched.[7]

Some proponents of choice argue that only enhanced parental voice and choice will provide a chance for educational salvation for minority parents and children.[8] Moe, for instance, claims that the best hope for the poor to gain the right 'to leave bad schools and seek out good ones' is through an 'unorthodox alliance.'[9] Only by allying themselves with Republicans and business – the most powerful groups supposedly willing to transform the system – can the poor succeed.

As I and others have shown elsewhere, there is growing empirical evidence that the development of quasi-markets in education has led to the exacerbation of existing social divisions surrounding class and race.[10] There are now increasingly convincing arguments that while the supposed overt goal of voucher and choice plans is to give poor people the right to exit public schools, among the ultimate long term effects may be to increase white flight from public schools into private and religious schools and to create the conditions where affluent white parents may refuse to pay taxes to support public schools that are more and more suffering from the debilitating effects of the fiscal crisis of the state. The result is even more educational apartheid, not less.[11]

There is a second variant of neo-liberalism. This one is willing to spend more state and/or private money on schools, if and only if schools meet the needs expressed by capital. Thus, resources are made available for reforms and policies that further connect the education system to the project of making our economy more competitive. Two examples can provide a glimpse of this position. In a number of states, legislation has been passed that directs schools and universities to make closer links between education and the business community. In the state of Wisconsin, for instance, all teacher education programmes have had to include identifiable experiences on education for employment for all of its future teachers; and all teaching in the public elementary, middle, and secondary schools of the state has had to include elements of education for employment in its formal curricula.

The second example is seemingly less consequential, but in reality it is a powerful statement of the reintegration of educational policy and practice into the ideological agenda of neo-liberalism. I am referring here to Channel One, a for-profit television network that is now being broadcast into schools, enrolling over 40% of all middle and secondary school students in the nation (many of which are financially hard-pressed given the fiscal crisis, even though many states are currently experiencing budget surpluses). In this reform, schools are offered a free satellite dish, two VCRs, and television monitors for each of their classrooms by a private media corporation. They are also offered a free news broadcast for these students. In return for the equipment and the news, all participating schools must sign a three to five year contract guaranteeing that their students will watch Channel One every day.

This sounds relatively benign. However, not only is the technology hard-wired so that only Channel One can be received, but broadcast along with the news are mandatory advertisements for major fast food, athletic wear, and other corporations that students – by contract – must also watch. Students, in essence, are sold as a captive audience to corporations. Since, by law, these students must be in schools, the US is one of the first nations in the world consciously to allow its youth to be sold as commodities to those many corporations willing to pay the high price of advertising on Channel One to get a guaranteed captive audience. Thus, under a number of variants of neo-liberalism not only are schools transformed into market commodities, but so too now are our children.

Neo-Conservatism: Teaching Real Knowledge
While neo-liberals largely are in leadership in the conservative alliance, I noted that the second major element within the new alliance is neo-conservatism. Unlike the neo-liberal emphasis on the weak state, neo-conservatives are usually guided by a vision of the strong state. This is especially true surrounding issues of knowledge, values, and the body. Whereas neo-liberalism may be seen as being

based in what Raymond Williams would call an 'emergent' ideological assemblage, neo-conservatism is grounded in 'residual' forms.[12] It is largely, though not totally, based in a romantic appraisal of the past, a past in which 'real knowledge' and morality reigned supreme, where people 'knew their place,' and where stable communities guided by a natural order protected us from the ravages of society.[13]

Among the policies being proposed under this ideological position are mandatory national and state-wide curricula, national and state-wide testing, a return to higher standards, a revivification of the Western tradition, patriotism, and conservative variants of character education. Yet, underlying some of the neo-conservative thrust in education and in social policy in general is not only a call for return. Behind it as well – and this is essential – is a fear of the Other. This is expressed in its support for a standardised national curriculum, its attacks on bilingualism and multiculturalism, and its insistent call for raising standards.

That the neo-conservative emphasis on a return to traditional values and morality has struck a responsive chord can be seen in the fact that among the best selling books in the nation during the past decade was William Bennett's *The Book of Virtues*.[14] Bennett, a former Secretary of Education in a conservative Republican administration, has argued that for far too long, 'We have stopped doing the right things [and] allowed an assault on intellectual and moral standards.' In opposition to this, we need 'a renewed commitment to excellence, character, and fundamentals.'[15] Bennett's book aims at providing moral tales for children to restore a commitment to traditional virtues such as patriotism, honesty, moral character, and entrepreneurial spirit. Not only have such positions entered the common sense of society in quite influential ways, but they have provided part of the driving force behind the movement toward charter schools. These are schools that have individual charters that allow them to opt out of most state requirements and develop curricula based on the wishes of their clientele. While in theory there is much to commend such policies, as a number of researchers have demonstrated, all too many charter schools have become ways through which conservative religious activists and others gain public funding for schools that would otherwise be prohibited such support.[16]

Behind much of this is a clear sense of loss – a loss of faith, of imagined communities, of a nearly pastoral vision of like minded people who shared norms and values and in which the Western tradition reigned supreme. It is more than a little similar to Mary Douglas's discussion of purity and danger, in which what was imagined to exist is sacred and 'pollution' is feared above all else.[17] We/they binary oppositions dominate this discourse and the culture of the Other is to be feared.

This sense of cultural pollution can be seen in the increasingly virulent attacks on multiculturalism (which is itself a very broad category that combines multiple political and cultural positions),[18] on the offering of schooling or any other social benefits to the children of illegal immigrants, and even in some cases to the children of legal immigrants, in the conservative English-only movement, and in the equally conservative attempts to reorient curricula and textbooks toward a particular construction of the western tradition.

Of course, such conservative positions have been forced into a kind of compromise in order to maintain their cultural and ideological leadership as a movement to reform educational policy and practice. A prime example is the emerging discourse over the history curriculum – in particular the construction of the United States as a 'nation of immigrants.'[19] In this hegemonic discourse, everyone in the history of the nation was an immigrant, from the first Native American population who supposedly trekked across the Bering Strait and ultimately populated North, Central, and South America, to the later waves of populations who came from Mexico, Ireland, Germany, Scandinavia, Italy, Russia, Poland and elsewhere, and finally to the recent populations from Asia, Latin America, Africa, and other regions. While it is true that the United States is constituted by people from all over the world – and that is one of the things that makes it so culturally rich and vital – such a perspective constitutes an erasure of historical memory. For some groups came *in chains* and were subjected to state sanctioned slavery and apartheid for hundreds of years. Others suffered what can only be called bodily, linguistic, and cultural destruction.

Yet it is not only in such things as the control over legitimate knowledge where neo-conservative impulses are seen. The idea of a strong state is also visible in the growth of the regulatory state as it concerns teachers. There has been a steadily growing change from 'licensed autonomy' to 'regulated autonomy' as teachers' work is more highly standardised, rationalised, and policed.[20] Under conditions of licensed autonomy, once teachers are given the appropriate professional certification they are basically free – within limits – to act in their classrooms according to their judgement. Such a régime is based on trust in professional discretion. Under the increasing conditions of regulated autonomy, teachers' actions are now subject to much greater scrutiny in terms of process and outcomes. Indeed, there are states in the US that have specified not only the content that teachers are to teach, but also have regulated the only appropriate methods of teaching. Not following these specified 'appropriate' methods puts the teacher at risk of administrative sanctions. Such a régime of control is based not on trust, but on a deep suspicion of the motives and competence of teachers. For neo-conservatives it is the equivalent of the notion of 'producer capture' that is so powerful among neo-liberals. For the former, however, it is not the market that will solve this problem, but a strong and interventionist state that will see to it that only 'legitimate' content and methods are taught. And this will be policed by state-wide and national tests of both students and teachers.

I have claimed elsewhere that such policies lead to the de-skilling of teachers, the intensification of their work, and the loss of autonomy and respect. This is not surprising, since behind much of this conservative impulse is a clear distrust of teachers and an attack both on teachers' claims to competence and especially on teachers' unions.[21] The mistrust in teachers, the concern over a supposed loss of cultural control, and the sense of dangerous pollution are among the many cultural and social fears that drive neo-conservative policies. However, as I noted earlier, underpinning these positions is often an ethnocentric, and even racialised, understanding of the world. Perhaps this can be best illuminated through the example of Herrnstein and Murray's volume, *The Bell Curve*.[22] In a book that sold hundreds of thousands of copies, the authors argue for a genetic determinism based on race, and to some extent gender. For them, it is romantic to assume that educational and social policies can ultimately lead to more equal results, since differences in intelligence and achievement are basically genetically driven. The wisest thing policy makers can do will be to accept this and plan for a society that recognises these biological differences and does not provide false hopes to the poor and the less intelligent, most of whom will be black. Obviously, this book has reinforced racist stereotypes that have long played a considerable part in educational and social policies in the United States.[23]

Authoritarian Populism: Schooling as God Wanted It

It is not possible to understand educational politics in the United States without paying a good deal of attention to the Christian Right. It is exceptionally powerful and influential, beyond its numbers, in debates over public policy in the media, education, social welfare, the politics of sexuality and the body, religion, and so on. Its influence comes from the immense commitment by activists within it, its large financial base, its populist rhetorical positions, and its aggressiveness in pursuing its agenda. New Right authoritarian populists ground their positions on education and social policy in clear visions of Biblical authority, Christian morality, gender roles, and the family. The New Right sees gender and the family, for instance, as an organic and divine unity that resolves male egoism and female selflessness.

As Hunter puts it:

> Since gender is divine and natural...there is [no] room for legitimate political conflict... Within the family women and men – stability and dynamism – are harmoniously fused when undisturbed by modernism, liberalism, feminism, and humanism which not only threaten masculinity and femininity directly, but also [do so] through their effects on children and youth... 'Real women,' i.e., women who know themselves as wives *and* mothers, will not threaten the sanctity of the home by striving for self. When men or women challenge these gender roles they break with God and nature; when liberals, feminists, and secular humanists prevent them from fulfilling these roles they undermine the divine and natural supports upon which society rests.[24]

In the minds of such groups, public schooling thus is *itself* a site of immense danger. In the words of conservative activist Tim LaHaye, 'Modern public education is the most dangerous force in a child's life: religiously, sexually, economically, patriotically, and physically.'[25] This is connected to the New Right's sense of loss surrounding schooling and the family.

> Until recently, as the New Right sees it, schools were extensions of home and traditional morality. Parents could entrust their children

11

to public schools because they were locally controlled and reflected Biblical and parental values. However, taken over by alien, elitist forces, schools now interpose themselves between parents and children. Many people experience fragmentation of the unity between family, church, and school as a loss of control of daily life, one's children, and America. Indeed, [the New Right] argues that parental control of education is Biblical, for in God's plan, the primary responsibility for educating the young lies in the home and directly in the father.[26]

It is exactly this sense of alien and elite control, the loss of Biblical connections, and the destruction of God-given family and moral structures that drives the authoritarian populist agenda. It is an agenda that is increasingly powerful, not only rhetorically, but in terms of funding and in conflicts over what schools should do, how they should be financed, and who should control them. This agenda includes, but goes beyond issues of gender, sexuality, and the family. It extends as well to a much larger array of questions about what is to count as legitimate knowledge in schools. And in this larger arena of concern about the entire *corpus* of school knowledge, conservative activists have had no small measure of success in pressuring textbook publishers to change what they include and in altering important aspects of state educational policy on teaching, curriculum, and evaluation. This is crucial, since in the absence of an overt national curriculum the commercially produced *textbook* – regulated by individual state's purchases and authority – remains the dominant definition of the curriculum in the United States.

The power of these groups is visible, for example, in the self-censorship in which publishers engage. For instance, under conservative pressure a number of publishers of high school literature anthologies have chosen to include Martin Luther King's 'I Have a Dream' speech, but only after all references to the intense racism of the United States have been removed.[27] At the level of state curriculum policy, this is very visible in the textbook legislation in Texas which mandates texts that stress patriotism, obedience to authority, and the discouragement of deviance.[28] Since most textbook publishers aim the content and organisation of their textbooks at what will be approved by a small number of populous states that in essence approve and purchase their textbooks *statewide*, this gives states like Texas and California immense power in determining what will count as official knowledge throughout the entire country.

12

Thus, in concert with neo-conservative elements within the conservative alliance, authoritarian populist religious activists have had a substantial influence on curriculum policy and practice. For them, only by re-centering issues of authority, morality, family, church, and decency can schools overcome the moral decay so evident all around us. Only by returning to inerrantist understandings of Biblical teachings and fostering or mandating a climate in schools where such teachings are given renewed emphasis, can our culture be saved.[29]

While a number of states and school systems have been able to create mechanisms that deflect some of these pressures, as I show in *Cultural Politics and Education* and *The State and the Politics of Knowledge,* the bureaucratic nature of many school systems and of the local and regional state in general has actually produced the conditions where parents and other community members, who might otherwise disagree with the New Right ideologically, are persuaded to join them in their attacks on the content and organisation of schooling.

While authoritarian populist struggles over curriculum and texts have been growing rapidly, this mistrust of public schools has also fuelled considerable and intense support among them for neo-liberal policies such as voucher and choice plans. The New Right, as a largely populist assemblage, has real mistrust of the motives and economic plans of capital. After all, such rightist populists have themselves experienced the effects of down-sizing, lay-offs, and economic restructuring. However, even given their partial insights into the differential effects of global competition and economic restructuring, they see in proposals for educational marketisation and privatisation a way in which they can use such reforms for their own purposes. Either through reduced school taxes, through tax credits, or through the allocation of public money to private and religious schools, they can create a set of schools organised around the more moral imagined communities they believe have been lost.

This search for the reconstitution of imagined communities points to one of the effects of reprivatisation talk on the politics surrounding educational policy. In the process of denying the legitimacy of oppositional claims, reprivatisation discourses may actually tend to politicise the issues even more. These issues become even more a part of public, not domestic, contestation. This paradox – reprivatisation talk may actually lead to further public discussion of breakaway needs – does not, however, always lead to victories by oppositional groups such as feminists, racially subjected peoples, or other disempowered groups. Rather, such politicisation can in fact lead to the growth of new social movements and new social identities whose fundamental aim is to push breakaway needs back into the economic, domestic, and private spheres. New, and quite conservative, coalitions can be formed.

This is exactly what has happened in the United States, where a set of re-privatising discourses in the accents of authoritarian populism has made creative connections with the hopes and especially the fears of a range of disaffected constituencies and has united them into a tense but very effective alliance supporting positions behind re-privatisation.[30] And this could not have been done if rightist groups had not succeeded in changing the very meaning of key concepts of democracy in such a way that the Christian Right could comfortably find a place under the larger umbrella of the conservative alliance.

The Professional and Managerial New Middle Class: More Testing, More Often

Members of the upwardly mobile professional and managerial new middle class do not all necessarily believe in the ideological positions that underpin the conservative alliance. In fact in other aspects of their lives they may be considerably more moderate and even liberal politically. However, as experts in efficiency, management, testing, and accountability, they provide the technical expertise to put in place the policies of conservative modernisation. Their own mobility *depends* on the expansion of both such expertise and the professional ideologies of control, measurement, and efficiency that accompany it. Thus, they often support such policies as neutral instrumentalities, even when these policies may be used for purposes other than the supposedly neutral ends this class fraction is committed to.

Yet, in a time when competition for credentials and cultural capital is intense, the increasing power of mechanisms of restratification such as the return of high levels of mandatory standardisation also provides mechanisms that enhance the chances that the children of the professional and managerial new middle class will have *less competition* from other children. Thus, the introduction of devices to restratify a population enhances the value of the credentials that the new middle class is more likely to accumulate, given the stock of cultural capital it already possesses.[31]

14

In such a situation, I believe that this group is not immune to ideological shifts to the Right. Given the fear generated by the attacks on the state and on the public sphere by both neo-liberals and neo-conservatives, this class fraction is decidedly worried about the future mobility of its children in an uncertain economic world. Thus, they may be drawn more overtly to parts of the conservative alliance's positions, especially those coming from the neo-conservative elements which stress greater attention to traditional high status content, greater attention to testing, and a greater emphasis on schooling as a stratifying mechanism. This can be seen in a number of states where parents of this class fraction are supporting charter schools that will stress academic achievement in traditional subjects and traditional teaching practices. It remains to be seen where the majority of members of this class grouping will align in the future in the debates over policy. Given their contradictory ideological tendencies, it is possible that the right will be able to mobilise them under conditions of fear for the future of their jobs and children.

Conclusion

Because of the complexity of educational politics in the United States, I have devoted most of this chapter to an analysis of the conservative social movements that are having a powerful impact on debates over policy and practice in education and in the larger social arena. I have suggested that conservative modernisation in education is guided by a tense coalition of forces, some of whose aims partly contradict others. Once state-wide and/or national curricula and tests are put in place, comparative school by school data will be available and will be published in a manner similar to the league tables on school achievement published in England. Only when there is standardised content and assessment can the market be set free, since the consumer can then have objective data on which schools are succeeding and which schools are not. Market rationality, based on consumer choice, will ensure that the supposedly good schools will gain students and the bad schools will disappear.

I do not want to give the impression that these four elements under the hegemonic umbrella of this coalition are uncontested or always victorious. This is simply not the case. As a number of people have demonstrated, at the local level throughout the United States there are scores of counter-hegemonic programmes and possibilities. Many institutions of higher education, schools, and even entire school districts have shown remarkable resilience in the face of the concerted ideological attacks and pressures from conservative restorational groups. And many teachers, academics, community activists, and others have created and defended educational programmes that are both pedagogically and politically emancipatory.

Indeed, we are beginning to see cracks in the alliance's power in unanticipated ways. For example, a growing number of students in elementary, middle, and secondary schools are actively refusing to take the mandatory tests that many states have introduced. This action has been supported by groups of teachers, administrators, parents, and activists.[32] Clearly, there are things bubbling up from below the surface whose effects will be interesting.

Notes

This chapter is drawn from a much more extensive analysis in Michael W. Apple, *Educating the 'Right' Way: Markets, Standards, God, and Inequality* (New York: Routledge, 2001).

1   Michael W. Apple, *Educating the 'Right' Way* (New York: Routledge, 2001).
2.   I am drawing upon Roger Dale, 'The Thatcherite Project in Education,' *Critical Social Policy* 9 (Winter 1989/1990), pp.4-19. Because of the size and complexity of the United States, I cannot focus on all of the policy issues and initiatives now being debated or implemented. For further descriptions, see the chapters on policy research in William Pink and George Noblit, eds. *Continuity and Contradiction: The Futures of the Sociology of Education* (Cresskill, New Jersey: Hampton Press, 1995).
3   See Michael W. Apple, *Ideology and Curriculum*, second edition (New York: Routledge, 1990).
4   Stephen Ball, *Education Reform* (Philadelphia: Open University Press, 1994) and Apple, *Cultural Politics and Education* (New York. Teachers College Press).
5   Apple, M. *Teachers and Texts: A Political Economy of Class and Gender Relations in Education* (London: Routledge) pp.31-78 and Sandra Acker, 'Gender and Teachers' Work,' in Michael W. Apple, ed. *Review of Research in Education* Volume 21 (Washington: American Educational Research Association, 1995), pp.99-162. A number of the larger gender implications of neo-liberalism in education and the economy can be seen in Jacky Brine, *Under-Educating Woman; Globalising Inequality* (Philadelphia: Open University Press, 1992) and Madeleine Arnot, Miriam David, and Gaby Weiner, *Closing the Gender Gap: Postwar Education and Social Change* (Cambridge, England: Polity Press, 1999).
6   John Chubb and Terry Moe, *Politics, Markets, and America's Schools* (Washington: Brookings Institution, 1990). See also, Ernest House, Schools for Sale (New York: Teachers College Press, 1998).
7   See Amy Stuart Wells, *Time to Choose* (New York: Hill and Wang, 1993), Jeffrey Henig, *Rethinking School Choice* (Princeton: Princeton University Press, 1994), Kevin Smith and Kenneth Meier, eds. *The Case Against School Choice* (Armonk, New York:

Michael W. Apple

M.E. Sharpe, 1995), Bruce Fuller, Elizabeth Burr, Luis Huerta, Susan Puryear and Edward Wexler, *School Choice: Abundant Hopes, Scarce Evidence of Results* (Berkeley and Stanford: Policy Analysis for California Education, University of California at Berkeley and Stanford University, 1999), and John F. Witte, *The Market Approach to Education* (Princeton: Princeton University Press, 2000).

8   Geoff Whitty, 'Creating Quasi-Markets in Education,' in Michael W. Apple, *Review of research in Education* Volume 22 (Washington: American Educational research Association, 1997), p17. See also Chubb and Moe, *Politics, Markets, and America's Schools* and Gary Rosen, 'Are Schools Vouchers Un-American?' *Commentary* 109 (February 2000), pp.26-31.

9   Quoted in Whitty, 'Creating Quasi-Markets in Education,' p.17.

10 See, for example, Apple, *Educating the 'Right' Way*, Geoff Whitty, Sally Power, and David Halpin, *Devolution and Choice in Education* (Philadelphia: Open University Press, 1998) and Hugh Lauder and David Hughes, *Trading in Futures: Why Markets in Education Don't Work* (Philadelphia: Open University Press, 1999).

11 See Apple, M *Cultural Politics and Education,* New York: Teachers College Press, especially Chapter 4, for a description of the ways in which many current social and educational policies often widen racial gaps.

12 For further discussion of residual and emergent ideological forms, see Raymond Williams, *Marxism and Literature* (New York: Oxford University Press, 1977).

13 See Allen Hunter, *Children in the Service of Conservatism* (Madison: University of Wisconsin, Institute for Legal Studies, 1988) and Apple, M *Cultural Politics and Education* (New York: Teachers College Press).

14 William Bennett, *The Book of Virtues* (New York: Simon and Schuster, 1994).

15 William Bennett, *Our Children and Our Country* (New York: Simon and Schuster, 1988), pp.8-10.

16 See, for example, Amy Stuart Wells, *Beyond the Rhetoric of Charter School Reform* (Los Angeles: University of California at Los Angeles, Graduate School of Education and Information Studies, 1999).

17 Mary Douglas, *Purity and Danger* (London: Routledge and Kegan Paul, 1966).

18 See, for example, Cameron McCarthy and Warren Crichlow, (eds.) *Race, Identity and Representation in Education* (New York: Routledge, 1994).

19 Catherine Cornbleth and Dexter Waugh, *The Great Speckled Bird* (New York: St. Martin's Press, 1995).

20 This distinction is developed in more depth in Dale, R *The State and Education Policy* (Philadelphia: Open University Press).

21. See Apple, M (1995) *Education and Power,* London: Routledge and Apple, M *Teachers and Texts: A Political Economy of Class and Gender Relations in Education* (London: Routledge) and Sandra Acker, 'Gender and Teachers' Work,' in Michael W. Apple, ed. *Review of Research in Education* Volume 21 (Washington: American Educational Research Association, 1995).

22 Richard Herrnstein and Charles Murray, *The Bell Curve* (New York: Free Press, 1994).

23 See Michael Omi and Howard Winant, *Racial Formation in the United States*, second edition (New York: Routledge, 1994) and Steven Selden, *Inheriting Shame* (New York: Teachers College Press, 1999).

24 Hunter, J *Children in the Service of Conservatism* (New York: Basic Books, 1996) p.15.

25 *Ibid*, p.57.

26 *Ibid.* p.97

27 Delfattore, *What Johnny Shouldn't Read* (New Haven: Yale University Press) 1992, p.123.

28   *Ibid*, p.139.
29   See Delfattore, *What Johnny Shouldn't Read* (New Haven: Yale University Press 1992), p.123, Ralph Reed, *After the Revolution* (Dallas: Word Publishing, 1996), and Fritz Detwiler, *Standing on the Premises of God* (New York: New York University Press, 1999).
30   Fraser, *Unruly Practices: Power, Discourse and Gender in Contemporary Social Theory* (Cambridge: Polity Press, 1997, pp.172-173).
31   See Bourdieu, P (translated Nice, R) *Distinction: A Social Critique of the Judgement of Taste* (New York: Harvard, 1992), Pierre Bourdieu, *Homo Economicus* (Stanford: Stanford University Press, 1988), and Pierre Bourdieu, *The State Nobility* (Stanford: Stanford University Press, 1996).
32   See Jacques Steinberg, 'Blue Books Closed, Students Boycott Standardised Tests,' *The New York Times*, April 13, 2000, pp.A1, A22.

2

Fun, amusing, full of insights, but ultimately a reflection of anxious times: a critique of postmodernism as a force for resistance, social change and social justice

MIKE COLE

Mike Cole critiques the notion that postmodernism is a viable force for resistance against the impact of global capitalism and social inequality. He presents us with some stark details on world poverty and corporate control, and argues that Marxism offers the only workable solution to contemporary political and social problems. Cole's analysis of the effects of political and economic globalisation echoes Apple's critique of the 'new hegemonic blocs' in the opening chapter of this book, and his focus on the loss of political hope foreshadows Wrigley's discussion of hope and despair in the concluding chapter in this section.

Introduction

In this chapter I begin by taking a brief glimpse at the current state of global capitalism. I then look at the arguments of Elizabeth Atkinson[1] that postmodernism can be a force for resistance, social change and social justice. I suggest that such claims are illusory and make the case that Marxism offers the only viable resistance to global capitalism; and the only option in the pursuit of effective resistance, social change and social justice.

Atkinson (2002) addresses herself to some recent writings on educational theory from within the Marxist tradition: specifically Marxist critiques of postmodernism (e.g. Cole and Hill, 1995; Cole *et al.*, 1997; Hill *et al.* (eds.) 1999; Kelly *et al.*, 1999). Atkinson concentrates on our claims that one of the greatest problems with postmodernism is that it lacks an agenda for social change and social justice. Her argument is that, 'through the acceptance of uncertainty, the acknowledgement of diversity and the refusal to see concepts such as 'justice' or 'society' as fixed or as governed by unassailable 'truths" (Atkinson, 2002:73), postmodernism, far from lacking such an agenda, is, in fact, a powerful force for social change. More recently, Atkinson has argued that 'postmodern thinking provides rich material for a form of resistance ... and challenges the structures through which we collude' (2003: 1).

My argument is that while I agree that postmodernism can be fun and amusing, and can provide insights into certain forms of oppression (e.g. Hayes, 2003:37), it is not an effective form of resistance, nor is it conducive to the pursuit of social change or social justice; and that, in the context of global capitalism today, Marxism provides the only viable option in that pursuit. What follows should not be read as an attack on the theoretical integrity of Elizabeth Atkinson, nor on the sincerity of her politics. I fully respect both. However, I believe she has got it wrong. Writing the first draft of this chapter in Plymouth, which, I am told, in line with British support for US imperial hegemony, sent 15,000 service personnel to the Gulf out of the total British force of 40,000, has reinforced this belief.

Global Capitalism Today

I would like to begin with a few recent and current facts about the state of globalised capitalism in the United States, the United Kingdom and the 'developing world'. As far as the US is concerned, during the 1980s, the top 10 percent of families increased their average family income by 16 percent, the top 5 percent by 23 percent, and the top 1 percent by 50 percent. At the same time, the bottom 80 percent all lost something, with the bottom 10 percent losing 15 percent of their incomes (George, 2000, cited in McLaren and Pinkney-Pastrana, 2001:208). The official poverty rate rose from 11.7 per cent in 2001 to 12.1 per cent in 2002, while the number of poor increased also by

1.7 million to 34.6 million (US Census Bureau, September 24th 2003).

In the UK, the latest figures show that the wealthiest one percent own 22 percent of wealth, while the wealthiest 50 percent own 94 percent (*Social Trends*, 2003:111). This means that the poorest half of the population own only 6 percent of all wealth (Hill and Cole, 2001, p. 139). With respect to income, in Britain, the bottom fifth of people earn less that 10 per cent of disposable income and the top fifth over 40 per cent (*Social Trends*, 2002:97). Over one in five children in Britain do not have a holiday away from home once a year because their parents cannot afford it (*ibid*: 87).

As far as the 'developing world' is concerned, for two decades poverty in Africa and Latin America has increased, both in absolute and relative terms. Nearly half the world's population are living on less than $2 a day and one fifth live on just $1 a day (World Development Movement, 2001). The turning over of vast tracts of land to grow one crop for multinationals often results in ecological degradation, with those having to migrate to the towns living in slum conditions and working excessive hours in unstable jobs (Harman, 2000). There are about one hundred million abused and hungry 'street kids' in the world's major cities; slavery is re-emerging, and some two million girls from the age of five to fifteen are drawn into the global prostitution market (Mojab, 2001:118). It was estimated that over twelve million children under five would die from poverty-related illness in 2001 (World Development Movement, 2001). Approximately, one hundred million human beings do not have adequate shelter and 830 million people are not 'food secure', i.c. they are hungry (Mojab, 2001:118). It has been calculated that, if current trends persist, in the whole of Latin America apart from Chile and Colombia, poverty will continue to grow in the next ten years, at the rate of two more poor people per minute (Heredia, 1997, cited in McLaren, 2000:39).

In fact, the world is becoming polarised into central and peripheral economies, with the gap between rich and poor, between the powerful and the powerless, growing so large that, by the late 1990s, the 300 largest corporations in the world accounted for 70 percent of foreign direct investment and 25 percent of world capital assets (Bagdikan, 1998, cited in McLaren, 2000:xxiv). At the start of the twenty-first century, the combined assets of the 225 richest people is roughly equal to the annual incomes of the poorest 47 percent of the world's population (Heintz and Folbre, 2000, cited in McLaren and Farahmandpur, 2001: 345) and eight companies earned more than half the world's population (World Development Movement, 2001).

Today, 125 million children cannot go to school and 110 million children, young people and adults have to leave school before they have completely acquired the basic skills of reading and writing. At the same time, the global education market is estimated to be worth more than 3,000 billion Euros (National Union of Education, Research and Culture, General Confederation of Labour, France 2002:4). As if to underline these massive global injustices, and as an indication of the amount of disposable capital available for states in the capitalist west, the United States is spending £8 million per day and Britain £5 million per day on the occupation of Iraq (The *Guardian*, 17th July 2003).

Responsible Anarchism

If postmodernism can be a force for resistance and for social change and social justice, then one would assume that it could in some way redress these global injustices. Atkinson (2002) begins her arguments by advocating Stronach and MacLure's (1997) concept of the postmodernist as 'a responsible anarchist'. They, in turn, borrowed this 'anarchic position' from Schurmann (1990) in an attempt to argue that the 'acceptance of disorder should not be mistaken for passivity or acquiescence' (Stronach and MacLure, 1997:98). Responsible anarchism involves 'standing against the fantasies of grand narratives, recoverable pasts, and predictable futures' (Stronach and MacLure, cited in Atkinson, 2002:73-4). I will take these propositions in turn. First, as I will argue later, I believe grand narrative Marxism, albeit amenable to critical interrogation, is essential in the promotion of social justice. Second, as far as 'recoverable pasts' are concerned, I would suggest that, while it is not possible nor necessarily desirable to return to the past *per se*, there have been events in the past from which we can learn as we plan for the future. Third, with respect to 'predictable futures', Marxists do not *predict* the future but merely have a vision of how societies *could* be run.

Mike Cole

Truth and Social Justice

Citing Jane Flax (1992), Atkinson argues that postmodernism calls into question 'the discovery of some sort of truth which can tell us how to act in the world in ways that benefit or are for the (at least ultimate) good of all' (2002:75). This is reminiscent of Derrida's assertion that 'truth is plural' (1979:103), the implication being that the 'truth' of the exploiter is equally as valid as the 'truth' of the exploited. For Derrida, 'difference' is in each and not between the two. While I would agree that knowing the 'truth' is not a question of describing some 'true' ontological essence, it is also not a function of an endless round of language games, as some would lead us to believe (e.g. Lyotard: 1984). A Marxist analysis of truth rejects both plurality and ontological essentialism in favour of 'a dialectical understanding of the dynamic relations between superstructure and base; between ideology ... and the workings of the forces of production and the historical relations of production' (Ebert, 1996:47; for an analysis, see Allman, 1999:136).

Referring specifically to the *concept* of 'justice', Atkinson states that 'postmodern theorists ... invite us to consider concepts such as 'justice' as 'effects of power' (2002:75). 'Social justice agendas', she implies, need to be deconstructed in order to reveal 'their own underlying assumptions and beliefs' (*ibid*). No Marxist would, of course, disagree with this (something which Atkinson acknowledges (*ibid*). The underlying assumptions and beliefs in the concept of 'justice' as employed by, for example, George W. Bush or Tony Blair, is very different from that employed by Noam Chomsky or John Pilger.

Whether or not Marx had a theory of justice has been an issue of great controversy and has generated an enormous literature. For a discussion, and arguments that a theory of social justice is, in fact, inherent in Marx, see Callinicos, 2000; see also Cole, 2001, 2003b. The main point, however, is that whatever Marx's relationship to the concept of social justice, interpreting the world, for him, was less important than changing it (Marx, 1976a:123). Whereas postmodernists engage in an endless and ahistorical process of deconstruction (see below), Marxists look to history to understand both underlying assumptions with respect to social justice and *solutions to social injustice*. A fundamental premise of Marxism is that change will not be brought about by appeals to social justice, but only by workers'

23

struggles. Another fundamental premise is that the capitalist state, a complex of institutions rather than just central government, is not neutral but acts to varying degrees, albeit with some disarticulations, in the interests of capitalism (Cole, 2001:73-4). The state must, therefore, be replaced rather than reformed.

Deconstruction and Social Change

Whereas for Marxists, the possibility of postmodernism leading to social change is a non sequitur, for Atkinson, postmodernism is 'an inevitable agent for change' in that

> it challenges the educator, the researcher, the social activist or the politician not only to deconstruct the certainties around which they might see as standing in need of change, but also to deconstruct their own certainties as to why they hold this view. (2002:75)

This sounds fine, but what do these constituencies actually *do* to effect meaningful societal change once their views have been challenged? What is *constructed* after the deconstruction process? Atkinson provides no answer. This is because postmodernism is incapable of providing an answer (Hill, 2001; Rikowski, 2002:20-25; Hill, 2003). Deconstruction 'seeks to do justice to all positions ... by giving them the chance to be justified, to speak originally for themselves and be chosen rather that enforced' (Zavarzadeh, 2002:8). Indeed, for Derrida (1990, cited in Stronach and MacLure, 1997: 33), 'deconstruction *is* justice' (my emphasis). Thus, once the deconstruction process has started, justice is already apparent and there is no discernible direction in which to head.

According to Atkinson, postmodernism 'does not have, and could not have, a 'single' project for social justice' (2002:75). Socialism then, if not social change, is thus ruled out in a stroke[2]. Atkinson then rehearses the familiar postmodern position on multiple projects (*ibid*).

The local and the global

Despite Atkinson's claims that postmodernism views 'the local as the product of the global and *vice versa*' and that postmodernism should not be interpreted as limiting its scope of enquiry to the local (2002: 81), since postmodernism rejects grand metanarratives and since it rejects universal struggle, it can, by *definition*, concentrate only on the local. Localised struggle can, of course, be empowering for individuals and certain selected small groups, but postmodernism cannot set out any viable mass strategy or programme for an emancipated future. The importance of local as well as national and international struggle is recognised by Marxists, but the postmodern rejection of mass struggle ultimately plays into the hands of those whose interests lie in the maintenance of national and global systems of exploitation and oppression. Furthermore, 'as regards aims, the concern with autonomy, in terms of organisation', postmodernism comprises 'a tendency towards network forms, and, in terms of mentality, a tendency towards self-limitation' (Pieterse, 1992). While networking can aid in the promotion of solidarity, and in mass petitions (Atkinson, 2001), it cannot replace mass action, in the sense of a general or major strike, or a significant demonstration or uprising which forces social change. Indeed, the postmodern depiction of mass action as totalitarian negates such action.

Non-dualism and socialism

Allied to its localism is postmodernism's non-dualism. This does have the advantage of recognising the struggles of groups oppressed on grounds in addition to, or other than, those of class. However, non-dualism prevents the recognition of a major duality in capitalist societies, that of social class (Cole and Hill, 1995:166-168; 2002; McLaren and Farahmandpur, 1999; Sanders *et al.*, 1999; Hill *et al.*, 2002). This has, I believe, profoundly reactionary implications, in that it negates the notion of class struggle.

Marxism, on the other hand, allows a future both to be envisioned and worked towards. This vision can and has been extended beyond the 'brotherhood of man' concept of early socialists, to include the complex subjectivities of all, subjectivities which the postmodernists are so keen to bring centre stage. Socialism can and should be conceived of as a project where subjective identities, such as gender, race, disability, non-exploitative sexual preference and age all have high importance in the struggle for genuine equality (Cole and Hill, 1999: 42)[3].

In her attempt to present the case that 'postmodern deconstruction ... is not the same as destruction' (2002:77), Atkinson cites Judith Butler (1992) who argues:

> To deconstruct is not to negate or to dismiss, but to call into question and, perhaps most importantly, to open up a term ... to a reusage or redeployment that previously has not been authorised. (cited in Atkinson, *ibid*)

This is precisely what Marxism does. The difference is that Marxist concepts such as the fetishism inherent in capitalist societies, in which the relationships between things or commodities assume a mystical quality, hiding the real exploitative relationships between human beings, provide a means of both analysing that society, understanding its exploitative nature *and* pointing in the direction of a non-exploitative society. The Marxist concept of the Labour Theory of Value is a good example (see below for a discussion).

Addressing herself to resistance to the ludicrous rhetoric of standards, improvement and best practice in British educational policy, Atkinson feels that she was born too late for 'full-blown Marxism' and acknowledges that while postmodernism has come only recently to education, it is not a new phenomenon in other fields (2003:4). Postmodernism can act as a form of resistance, Atkinson argues, by pitting its 'ludic ... playful ... ironic ... restless, shape-shifting dance ... against the ludicrous' (*ibid*: 5) – in this case, current British educational policy. While laughing at the ludicrous is OK for starters, Atkinson wants to hear the voices from the margins, to resist 'binary oppositions' and 'either/ or thinking' (*ibid*: 8) in order that she may think again and again (*ibid*: 12). Here, in true postmodern style, Atkinson appears to be attempting to combine ludic and resistance postmodernism as part of a progressive project. Others (e.g. Lather, 1991: 160-161) see ludic and resistance postmodernisms as discrete entities, the former reactionary, the latter progressive. Still others (e.g. Cole and Hill, 2002: 90-92) see 'the two' as lying on one continuum and view postmodernism as a whole to be essentially reactionary.

For Marxists, 'either/or' thinking is essential now more than ever before. As we move towards a world order, where United States imperialism, aided by Britain, attempts to impose its own version of capitalism on the world by force, it is time to think of a concrete alternative. To reiterate, a return to a more benign form of capitalism (in so far as capitalism is capable of being benign), is not on the agenda. World socialism is the only known alternative. To quote an old socialist adage, it really is a choice between barbarism or socialism.

26

Conclusion

Atkinson's main argument seems to be that the strength of post-modernism is that it 'comes as something of a shock' (2002:78) and reveals sub-texts and textual silences (*ibid*). Well, so does Marxism on both counts. The difference is that with the former, after our shock, there is not much else to do, except at the local level. One of the great strengths of Marxism is that it allows us to move beyond appearances and to look beneath the surface *and* to move forward. Marx's Labour Theory of Value (LTV), for example, explains most concisely why capitalism is objectively a system of exploitation, whether the exploited realise it or not, or indeed, whether they believe it to be an issue of importance for them or not. The LTV also provides a *solution* to this exploitation. It thus provides *dialectical* praxis – the authentic union of theory and practice.

The labour theory of value

According to the LTV, the interests of capitalists and workers are diametrically opposed, since the benefit to the former of profits is a cost to the latter (Hickey, 2002:168). Marx argued that workers' labour is embodied in goods that they produce. The finished products are appropriated by the capitalists and eventually sold at a profit. However, the worker is paid only a fraction of the value s/he creates in productive labour; the wage does not represent the *total* value s/he creates. We *appear* to be paid for every single second we work. However, underneath this appearance, this fetishism, the working day as under serfdom is split in two: into socially necessary labour represented by the wage and surplus labour, labour not reflected in the wage. This is the basis of surplus value, out of which comes the capitalist's profit. While the value of the raw materials and of the depreciating machinery is simply passed on to the commodity in production, labour power is a peculiar, indeed unique commodity, in that it creates new value. 'The magical quality of labour-power's ... value for ... capital is therefore critical' (Rikowski, 2001:11). 'Labour-power creates more value (profit) in its consumption than it possesses itself, and than it costs' (Marx, 1966:351). Unlike, for example, the value of a given commodity, which can only be realised in the market as itself, labour creates a new value, a value greater than itself, a value which previously did not exist. It is for this reason that labour power is so important for the capitalist, in the quest for capital accumulation. It is in the interest of the capitalist or capitalists (nowadays, capitalists consist of a number of shareholders, rather than outright owners of businesses) to maximise profits which entails (in order to create the greatest amount of new value) keeping workers' wages as low as is 'acceptable' in any given country or historical period, without provoking effective strikes or other forms of resistance. Therefore, the capitalist mode of production is, in essence, a system of exploitation of one class, the working class, by another, the capitalist class.

Whereas class conflict is endemic to, and ineradicable and perpetual within the capitalist system, it does not typically take the form of open conflict or expressed hostility (Hickey, 2002:168). Fortunately for the working class, however, capitalism is prone to cyclical instability and to periodic political and economic crises. At these moments, the possibility exists for socialist revolution. Revolution can only come about when the working class, in addition to being a 'class-in-itself' (an *objective* fact because of the shared exploitation inherent as a result of the LTV) becomes 'a class-for-itself' (Marx, 1976b). By this, Marx meant a class with a *subjective* awareness of its social class position, a class with 'class consciousness', including its awareness of its exploitation and its transcendence of 'false consciousness'.

Marx argued that if and when the working class has become a 'class-for-itself', it has the potential to seize control of the means of production, the economy, and take political power. Seizure of the economy would constitute such a socialist revolution (Hill and Cole, 2001: 147). This, of course, is not an easy option, but it is the working class that is most likely to be at the forefront of such a revolution.

As Michael Slott has so clearly put it:

> Marxists have understood perfectly well that there are many obstacles to the working class becoming a universal agent for socialism. At the same time, Marxists have argued that, because of the particular interests, collective power, and creative capacities that are generated by workers' structural position in society, the working class is more likely to be at the core of any movement of social transformation. (2002:419)

Bringing back Marxism

For Marx, socialism (a stage before communism – that state of existence when the state would wither away and we would live com munally) was a world system in which 'we shall have an association, in which the free development of each is the condition for the free development of all' (Marx and Engels, 1977:53). Marx and Engels attempted to learn from the experiences of the Paris Commune of 1871 in their Preface to the German Edition (1872) [1977] of the *Manifesto of the Communist Party*. In fact, the whole Marxist project is based on the belief that history is progressive. Thus, for example, we can learn from the earliest forms of primitive communism, but in the context of a dialectic of accumulative progressive change. Such a society would be democratic so that socialism as envisaged by Marx should be distanced from the *undemocratic* régimes of the former Soviet bloc and classless, and the means of production would be in the hands of the many, not the few. Goods and services would be produced for need and not for profit.

Postmodernists are clearly capable of asking questions – but by their own acknowledgement they have no answers. As Glenn Rikowski has put it, this leads one to ask: just what is the postmodernist attitude to explanation?

> Truly political strategies require explanation (of what went wrong, why the analysis and/or tactics failed etc.) so that improvements can be made. Do postmodernists have a notion of improvement (of society, of political strategies)? If they do, then they need explanation. I don't think they are interested in either, and hence can't have a political strategy for human betterment. (Personal communication, cited in Cole, 2001:77)

To this I would reiterate that postmodernism could be empowering to individuals and to localised groups. But to be politically valid, an analysis must link 'the small picture' to 'the big picture'. Postmodernism, by its protagonists' acknowledgement, cannot do this. They are, thus, not merely unable to promote social justice and social change but by default act as ideological supports for capitalism, both within nation states and globally.

Bringing Marxism back to the forefront is not an easy task. Marxists must break through the 'bizarre ideological mechanism, [in which] *every* conceivable alternative to the market has been discredited by the collapse of Stalinism' (Callinicos, 2000:122), and the fetishisation of life makes capitalism seem natural and therefore unalterable and the market mechanism 'has been hypostatised into a natural force unresponsive to human wishes' (*ibid*:125). Here, we have a further ironic twist: the capitalist class and their representatives who used to deride what they saw as the metaphysic of 'Marxist economic determinism' are the ones who now champion the 'world-wide market revolution' and the accompanying *inevitability* of 'economic restructuring' (McMurtry, 2000; see also Cole, 1998; 2003a, c; 2004a). Capital presents itself 'determining the future as surely as the laws of nature make tides rise to lift boats (McMurtry, 2000:2), 'as if it has now replaced the natural environment. It announces itself through its business leaders and politicians as coterminous with freedom, and indispensable to democracy such that any attack on capitalism as exploitative or hypocritical becomes an attack on world freedom and democracy itself' (McLaren, 2000:32). At the same time, globalisation, in reality in existence since the beginnings of capitalism, is hailed as a new and unchallengeable phenomenon and its omnipresence used ideologically to further fuel arguments about capitalism's inevitability (Cole, 1998; 2003c; 2004a). As Callinicos puts it, despite the inevitable intense resistance from capital, the 'greatest obstacle to change is not ... the revolt it would evoke from the privileged, but the belief that it is impossible' (2000:128).

> Challenging this climate requires courage, imagination and willpower inspired by the injustice that surrounds us. Beneath the surface of our supposedly contented societies, these qualities are present in abundance. Once mobilised, they can turn the world upside down. (*ibid*:129)

To reiterate, postmodernism is indeed fun (Hayes, 2003:37; Atkinson 2003:7) and it can provide insights. However, Hayes is right that it is ultimately just a reflection of anxious times, rather than a serious contribution to educational thought (2003:37). Postmodernists, of course, claim insights beyond 'educational theory' and make statements applicable to much wider issues. As times get more anxious, as they surely will in the light of the invasion of Iraq and its aftermath, let us hope that the fun for those in the academy is transposed to a wider community. For this to happen, we will need to look to Marxism, for Marxism is about dialectical praxis. Such praxis is outside the remit of postmodernism, which is unable to address the global social injustices outlined at the beginning of this paper. By its very essence, postmodernism is about neither theory nor practice. It fails in both and remains an academic practice, based on deconstruction alone, with no practical implications for social or educational transformation. Indeed, deconstruction without reconstruction typifies the divorce of the academy from the reality of struggle on the ground.

Notes

1   This chapter draws heavily on previously published papers (Cole, 2001, 2003a) which engage in a critique of Atkinson's work. My critique focuses largely on Atkinson 2002, but also including some comments on her opening chapter in the first book of this series (Atkinson, 2003). For an extended critique of postmodernism and poststructuralism as forces for social change and social justice, including the work of Atkinson, see Cole (forthcoming, 2005)

2   Atkinson's response to this point first made in Cole (2001) was 'well, possibly Socialism with a capital S' (although I would suggest, 'considered as one of many possibilities' rather than 'ruled out" (Atkinson, 2001:90).

3   Class, however, remains central. This is demonstrated clearly by the current occupation of Iraq. While the conflict may be gendered and racialised in various ways, this invasion and occupation is ultimately about class and capitalism, and indeed, imperialism (Cole, 2004b): about the privatisation of basic services in Iraq; about the ownership and control of oil – in short, about increasing the global profits of capital at the expense of the working class, about squeezing out more and more surplus value from the labour of workers.

References

Allman, P (1999) *Revolutionary Social Transformation: Democratic hopes, political possibilities and critical education*. Westport, Connecticut: Bergin and Garvey

Atkinson, E (2001) A response to Mike Cole's 'Educational postmodernism, social justice and societal change: an incompatible ménage-a-trois', in *The School Field*, 12(1/2): 87-94

Atkinson, E (2002) The responsible anarchist: postmodernism and social change, in British Journal of Sociology of Education, 23(1): 73-87

Atkinson, E (2003) Education, postmodernism and the organisation of consent, in: Satterthwaite, J, Atkinson, E and Gale, K (eds) *Discourse, Power, Resistance: Challenging the rhetoric of contemporary education*. Stoke-on-Trent: Trentham Books

Bagdikan, B H (1998) Capitalism and the information age, in: *Monthly Review*, 50(7): 55-58

Callinicos, A (2000) *Equality*. Oxford: Polity

Cole, M (1998) Globalisation, modernisation and competitiveness: a critique of the New Labour project in education, in *International Studies in Sociology of Education*, 8(3): 315-332

Cole, M (2001) Educational postmodernism, social justice and societal change: an incompatible ménage-a-trois, in *The School Field*, 12(1/2): 69-85

Cole, M (2003a) Might it be in the practice that it fails to succeed? A Marxist critique of claims for postmodernism and poststructuralism as forces for social change and social justice, in *British Journal of Sociology of Education*, 24(4): 485-498

Cole, M (2003b) Global capital, postmodern/poststructural deconstruction and social change: a Marxist critique, available at http://www.nodo50.org/cubasigloXXI/congreso/cole_05abr03.pdf

Cole, M (2003c) The 'inevitability of globalised capital' vs. the 'ordeal of the undecidable': a Marxist critique, in: Pruyn, M (ed) *Teaching Peter McLaren: Paths of dissent.* New York: Peter Lang

Cole, M (2004a) New Labour, globalisation and social justice: the role of education, in: Fischman, G, McLaren, P, Sunker, H and Lankshear, C (eds) *Critical Theories, Radical Pedagogies and Global Conflicts.* Lanham, Maryland: Rowman and Littlefield

Cole, M (2004b forthcoming) 'Britons never never never shall be slaves': the role of imperialism in the British Education System, paper to be presented at the annual Discourse, Power, Resistance conference, Plymouth, UK, April

Cole, M (2005, forthcoming) *Marxism, Postmodernism and Education: Pasts, presents and futures.* London: Routledge/Falmer

Cole, M and Hill, D (1995) Games of despair and rhetorics of resistance: postmodernism, education and reaction, in: *British Journal of Sociology of Education*, 16(2): 165-18

Cole, M and Hill, D (1999) Into the hands of capital: the deluge of postmodernism and the delusions of resistance postmodernism, in: Hill, D, McLaren, P, Cole, M and Rikowski, G (eds) *Postmodernism in Educational Theory: Education and the politics of human resistance.* London: The Tufnell Press

Cole, M and Hill, D (2002) 'Resistance postmodernism' – progressive politics or rhetorical left posturing?, in: Hill, D, McLaren, P, Cole, M and Rikowski, G (eds) *Marxism against Postmodernism in Educational Theory.* Lanham, Maryland: Lexington Books

Cole, M, Hill, D and Rikowski, G (1997) Between postmodernism and nowhere: the predicament of the postmodernist, in: *British Journal of Educational Studies*, 45(2): 187-200

Derrida, J (1979) *Spurs: The styles of Nietzsche.* Chicago: University Of Chicago Press

Derrida, J (1992) Force of law: the mystical foundation of authority, in: Cornell, D, Rosenfeld, M and Carlson, D (eds) *Deconstruction and the Possibility of Justice.* London: Routledge

Ebert, T L (1996) *Ludic Feminism and After: Postmodernism, desire, and labor in late capitalism.* Ann Arbor: University Of Michigan Press

Flax, J (1992) The end of innocence, in: Butler, J and Scott, J (eds) *Feminists Theorise the Political.* New York: Routledge

Green, A (1994) Postmodernism and state education, in *Journal of Education Policy*, 9(1): 67-83

Harman, C (2000) Anti-capitalism: theory and practice, in: *International Socialism*, 88: 3-59

Mike Cole

Hayes, D (2003) New Labour, new professionalism, in: Satterthwaite, J, Atkinson, E and Gale, K (eds) *Discourse, Power, Resistance: Challenging the rhetoric of contemporary education*. Stoke-on-Trent: Trentham Books

Heintz, J and Folbre, N (2000) *The Ultimate Field Guide to the US Economy: A Compact and Irreverant Guide to Economic Life in America*. New York: New Press

Heredia, B (1997) Prosper or Perish? Development in the age of global capital, in: *Current History: A Journal of Contemporary World Affairs* (November): 383-388

Hickey, T (2002) Class and class analysis for the twenty-first century, in: Cole, M (ed) *Education, Equality and Human Rights*. London: Routledge/Falmer

Hill, D (2001) State theory and the neo-liberal reconstruction of schooling and teacher education: a structuralist neo-Marxist critique of postmodernist, quasi-postmodernist and culturalist neo-Marxist theory, in: *British Journal of Sociology of Education*, 22(1): 135-155

Hill, D (2003) The state and education, in: Fischman, G, McLaren, P, Sunker, H and Lankshear, C (eds) *Critical Theories, Radical Pedagogies and Global Conflicts*. Lanham, Maryland: Rowman and Littlefield

Hill, D and Cole, M (2001) Social class, in: Hill, D and Cole, M (eds) *Schooling and Equality: Fact, concept and policy*. London: Kogan Page

Hill, D, Sanders, M and Hankin, T (2002) Marxism, class analysis and post-modernism, in: Hill, D, McLaren, P, Cole, M and Rikowski, G (eds) (2002) *Marxism against Postmodernism in Educational Theory*. Lanham, Maryland: Lexington Books

Hill, D, McLaren, P, Cole, M and Rikowski, G (eds) (1999) *Postmodernism in Educational Theory: Education and the politics of human resistance*. London: The Tufnell Press

Hill, D, McLaren, P, Cole, M and Rikowski, G (eds) (2002) *Marxism Against Postmodernism In Educational Theory*. Lanham, Md: Lexington Books

Kelly, J, Cole, M and Hill, D (1999) Resistance postmodernism and the ordeal of the undecidable. Paper presented at the British Educational Research Association Annual Conference, Brighton, September

Lather, P (1991) *Getting Smart: Feminist research and pedagogy with/in the postmodern*. New York: Routledge

Lyotard, J-J (1984) *The Postmodern Condition: A report on knowledge*. Minneapolis: University of Minnesota Press

Marx, K (1966) [1894] *Capital, Vol 3*. Moscow: Progress Publishers

Marx, K (1976a) [1965] Theses On Feuerbach, in: Arthur, C J (ed) *Marx and Engels, The German Ideology*. London: Lawrence And Wishart

Marx, K (1976b) The eighteenth brumaire of Louis Bonaparte, in: Marx, K and Engels, F *Selected Works in One Volume*. London: Lawrence and Wishart

Marx, K And Engels, F (1977) [1872]. Preface to the German edition of the manifesto of the Communist Party, in: Marx, K and Engels, F *Selected Works in One Volume*. London: Lawrence And Wishart

McLaren, P (2000) *Che Guevara, Paulo Freire and the pedagogy of revolution*. Oxford: Rowman and Littlefield

McLaren, P and Farahmandpur, R (1999) Critical pedagogy, postmodernism and the retreat from class: towards a contraband pedagogy, in: Hill, D, McLaren, P, Cole, M and Rikowski, G (eds) *Postmodernism in Educational Theory: Education and the politics of human resistance*. London: The Tufnell Press

McLaren, P and Pinkney-Pastrana, J (2001) Cuba, yanquizacion, and the cult of Elian Gonzalez: a view from the 'Enlightened' States, in: *International Journal of Qualitative Studies in Education*, 14(2): 201-219

McMurtry, J (2001) Education, struggle and the Left today, in: *International Journal Of Educational Reform* 10(2): 145-162

Mojab, S (2001) New resources for revolutionary critical education, in: *Convergence* 34(1): 118-125

National Union of Education, Research and Culture, General Confederation Of Labour, France (2002) Untitled paper presented at the European Social Forum, Florence, 6-10 November

Pieterse, N (1992) *Emancipations, Modern and Postmodern*. London: Sage

Rikowski, G (2001) The importance of being a radical educator in capitalism today, Guest Lecture in Sociology of Education, Department of Sociology, University of Warwick, Coventry, 24 May, (available from Rikowski@ Tiscali.Co.Uk)

Rikowski, G (2002) Prelude: Marxist educational theory after postmodernism, in: Hill, D, McLaren, P, Cole, M and Rikowski, G (eds) (2002) *Marxism against Postmodernism in Educational Theory*. Lanham, Maryland: Lexington Books

Sanders, M, Hill, D and Hankin, T (1999) Education theory and the return to class analysis, in: Hill, D, McLaren, P, Cole, M and Rikowski, G (eds) *Postmodernism in Educational Theory: Education and the politics of human resistance*. London: The Tufnell Press

Schurmann, R (Tr Gross, C-M) (1990) *Heidegger on Being and Acting: From principles to anarchy*. Bloomington: Indiana University Press

Slott, M (2002) Does critical postmodernism help us 'name the system'? in: *British Journal of Sociology of Education*, 23(3): 414-425

Social Trends (2002) No. 32: Editors: Jil Matheson and Penny Babb. London: The Stationery Office

Social Trends (2003) No. 33: Editors: Carol Summerfield and Penny Babb. London: The Stationery Office

Stronach, I and MacLure, M (1997) *Educational Research Undone: The postmodern embrace*. Buckingham: Open University Press

US Census Bureau (2003) http://www.census.gov/Press-Release/www/releases/ archives/income_wealth/001371.html

World Development Movement (2001) *Isn't it Time we Tackled the Causes of Poverty?* London: World Development Movement

Zavarzadeh, M (2002) On 'class' and related concepts in classical Marxism, and why is the post-al Left saying such terrible things about them? Available at http://www.Etext.Org/Politics/Alternativeorange/3/V3n3_Onrc.Htm

3

School effectiveness and improvement – where is the grand narrative?

TERRY WRIGLEY

*Terry Wrigley examines the discourse of school effective-
ness and improvement, and in particular its surface optimism and earnestness, and the deep sense of scepticism
which flows beneath the surface. By deconstructing Effectiveness and Improvement, with particular reference to
quality and change, Wrigley aims to explore the ideological assumptions and popular tropes of these parallel discourses by asking what they systematically conceal. Whilst
exam results and qualifications are clearly of worth, the
emphasis on measurement may marginalise or displace
other educational aims in terms of social and personal
development. The chapter concludes by appealing for coherent explanations linking educational governance with
wider power structures.*

'Imagine a radical movement which had suffered an emphatic defeat.'
With this bold opening sentence to *The Illusions of Postmodernism*,
Terry Eagleton (1996) reveals a hidden coherence among its seemingly
disconnected strands: they are a set of displacements resulting from a
loss of hope that socialism is still possible. He takes us on a tour
through the luxuriant undergrowth of postmodernism, to find:

- an upsurge of interest in the margins and crevices of the system

- various veins of pseudo-mysticism

- something more intimate and immediate, more sensuous and particular [the body]

- the terrors and allures of the signifier, its snares, seductions and subversions, an ersatz iconoclasm in a politically quiescent society

- an enormous upsurge of interest in the alien, deviant, exotic, unincorporable (pp2-17)

Of course, while postmodern intellectuals were savouring the end of Enlightenment 'grand narrative', capitalism was resolutely pursuing one of its own – its ultimate narrative of globalisation and imperialism, culminating in Rumsfeld and Co's brazen declaration of a New American Century (www.newamericancentury.com).

* * *

Though the weighty literature of School Effectiveness and Improvement is nothing like as exotic as the tropical forests of postmodernism, its earnest empiricism is built on the very same foundation – a loss of political hope.

This may seem an absurd accusation to make against a policy régime which is oppressive precisely through its boundless insistence on 'improvement' – a discourse glowing with mission and vision, escalating targets and expectations, leadership which improves schools exponentially by increasing the capacity for change. Beneath the surface, however, we find a deep scepticism that genuine social transformation is possible.

In the words of its key defenders, the editors of the *International Handbook of School Effectiveness Research* (2000):

> The 'narrow agenda' of pragmatists working in SER [school effectiveness research] is more realistic at this point in time than the 'redistributive policies' of the critical theorists... Pragmatists, working within the SER paradigm, believe that efforts to alter the existing relationship between social class and student achievement by bringing about broad societal changes are *naïve, perhaps quixotic. We prefer to work within the constraints of the current social order.* (Teddlie and Reynolds, 2001: 70-71, my italics)

Here, while resolutely defending the Effectiveness paradigm, its principle gatekeepers reveal the contradiction at its heart – a despair masquerading as optimism, a deeply conservative radicalism.

The ideology of Effectiveness and Improvement

Since the Effectiveness literature is, in general, so resolutely apolitical, this fissure – the result of pressure from opponents, in a debate taken right into the pages of Teddlie and Reynold's own journal, is worthy of serious attention. School Effectiveness and School Improvement cannot be adequately understood within the logic of their own language games. The terms in which they frame issues of *quality* and *change* are marked with a determining + sign: *effective, improving*. The ideological impact of such positively occupied words begins with the sheer impossibility of disagreeing: you could no more wish to be 'ineffective' or reject the call to 'improve' a school, than you could disagree with personal hygiene or kindness to animals.

If we wish to understand *Effectiveness* and *Improvement* as particular versions of quality and change, we need to make the silences speak. Just as literary theorists discovered that the silences in texts could reveal as much as the words: the significant gaps, the textual slippages, the *deus ex macchina* endings, the stories they do not tell and the characters whose thoughts remain unvoiced. This paper seeks to explore the ideological orientation of these twin paradigms by asking what they systematically conceal.

School Effectiveness and School Improvement have become so dominant in some countries that it is easy to accept their claim to be global phenomena. For 'across the world', read 'across the English-speaking world'. In fact, they are only seriously hegemonic in Britain, particularly England, and the USA, parts of Canada and Australia, and a few Pacific Rim areas such as Taiwan and Hong Kong. Nevertheless, state demands for 'accountability' are spreading.

It is illuminating to look to the very different conceptions of school quality and school development in Western Europe to gain a different perspective.

> Whereas in German and French speaking countries, a quite broadly defined concept of 'quality' is prominent, the Anglo-Saxon countries prefer the narrower concept of 'effectiveness' which is empirically tangible but consequently limited to only a few of the effects of schooling. (Büeler, 1998:666)

The German literature insists on evaluating the quality of process, the ten or more years of our lives we spend in schools, as well as the product, and on making judgements about success which are grounded in debates about social and educational values. By contrast, Effectiveness and Improvement are overwhelmingly focused on the quantifiable outcomes of test and exam scores.

> Effective schooling and the school improvement movement is blind to a searching interrogation of outcome. Test scores become ends... Explicit discussions of values and the types of society to which schools articulate/adhere are ignored. (Slee, 1998:111)

School Effectiveness

Although School Effectiveness and School Improvement are often confused, a clear distinction can be drawn between the two paradigms. The first is a branch of statistics which attempts to quantify the impact of schooling compared with other factors in a child's life, and particularly to measure the differential effectiveness between schools once socio-economic factors are controlled for. The second is a process-based qualitative study of school development, focusing on culture, leadership and change management which, in the English-speaking world, has meekly followed School Effectiveness by tacitly accepting quantifiable outcomes as the true purpose of schooling.

This is not to say, of course, that examination results don't matter. They are an important indicator of school success, and qualifications can be crucially important for young people facing discrimination on the basis of their postcodes or skin colour. More precisely, I would like to insist that

- schooling has other important purposes (e.g. democracy, community, social justice, empathy, critical thinking)

- no evaluation can be valid without a debate about educational aims

- unless a range of issues contributing to social and personal development are taken seriously as ends in themselves, children growing up in marginalised communities are unlikely to succeed, even in the narrower terms of exam success.

I have argued elsewhere (Wrigley, 2003: 11-26) that School Effectiveness is reductionist in four senses:

- methodologically

38

- contextually

- historically

- morally or teleologically.

There is no space here to repeat that systematic critique, so I will focus on a few features which produce a significant ideological effect.

i) *The statistical methodology*

For many people, numbers create an aura of false objectivity. Beyond this, there are special features of School Effectiveness which serve to engender an unwarranted trust. An impression is created that an input factor such as 'strong leadership' emerges directly from the empirical data, whereas it is inevitably chosen by the project's lead researchers, eventually becoming part of the common sense assumptions of this field of research. A term such as 'strong leadership' is a floating signifier which could refer to anything from co-operative to dictatorial. It is subsequently open to politicians and officials to impose their own interpretations under cover of the statistical association with school success.

ii) *Sidelining social context*

School effectiveness research claims to take full account of socio-economic factors in its search for within-school factors which 'make a difference'. Ironically, Teddlie and Reynolds, in arguing that it does not 'ignore context variables', actually confirm the marginalisation of the social environment, Their very choice of words is indicative of a reduction of the rich texture of social and cultural life to a number.

The research process is a unidirectional one which foregrounds school factors while marginalising the social environment. As Angus (1993: 361) argues:

> Family background, social class, any notion of context are typically regarded as 'noise', as 'outside background factors' which must be controlled for and then stripped away so that the research can concentrate on the important domain of 'school factors'.

In reality, school processes of pedagogy, ethos and leadership do not operate in a vacuum, but constitute interactions between 'inside' and 'outside' cultures. Moreover, schools serving marginalised communities can only succeed by connecting themselves creatively with their communities while simultaneously contesting educationally harmful behaviours.

Overall, while appearing to take context into account, the School Effectiveness discourse inevitably serves to blame schools in the poorest areas. Even more sophisticated analyses based on 'value-addedness' assume that if attainment at age eleven is used as the baseline, all schools can then operate on a level playing field and 'add value' at a similar rate. In fact in England which is virtually a testbed for Effectiveness-based Improvement, although there is substantial overlap between attainment levels in the richest and poorest schools at age eleven, there is virtually none by age sixteen. Only 2% of schools with over 35% of pupils entitled to free school meals even reach the national average for five or more GCSE A*-C grades at age sixteen (Ofsted, 2000). The most 'effective' schools in the poorest areas struggle hard for their relative success, though the Effectiveness discourse suggests that absolute success can be achieved by dedication and technically efficient teaching.

iii) A paradigm in denial of history

The guardians of the Effectiveness paradigm see its origins in a rejection of the findings of the Coleman report (1966) on educational inequalities, published at the time of racial desegregation in the USA. This turning point is presented as if an arithmetical recalculation led to the abandonment of Sociology and its replacement by Effectiveness Research. Coleman's study was ground breaking in its insistence on the impact of racism and poverty on school achievement. Effectiveness researchers preferred to attack its conclusions as unduly pessimistic, even though their own figures rarely show schools having a bigger impact than social 'background'.

The leading effectiveness researchers are equally blind to the ways in which their own work is used and abused by politicians. Peter Mortimore has been almost alone among British effectiveness researchers in denouncing abuse of the research by governments who would clearly prefer to blame teachers than to take decisive steps to reduce poverty.

There is a parallel between the 'blame and shame' culture which effectiveness research helps to fuel and the Victorian myth of the 'self-made man':

> Any capitalist here, who had made sixty thousand pounds out of
> sixpence, always professed to wonder why the sixty thousand
> nearest Hands didn't each make sixty thousand pounds out of six-
> pence, and more or less reproached them everyone for not accom-
> plishing the little feat. What I did, you can do. Why don't you go
> and do it? (Dickens: Hard Times. 1854)

The sudden popularity of effectiveness research in England can only
be understood in terms of the dramatic socio-political transformation
under the Thatcher government, since reinforced by New Labour. The
quasi-market which placed schools in competition with each other,
the vagaries of parental choice, local competition and image building
had to be obscured by the seemingly objective superiority of 'more
effective' schools.

iv) A moral vacuum

The amoral and asocial politics of neo-liberalism found its counter-
part in the technical rationalism of the effectiveness discourse. There
was a need to silence, as far as possible, discussion about social purpose and values and to substitute a powerful régime of surveillance
based upon supposedly objective success criteria.

The replacement of 'good' by 'effective' made it seem unnecessary to
debate what we wanted schools to be *good for*? Moreover, *effectiveness* could be measured in terms of average attainment, without questioning which pupils were gaining and which were losing out because
of particular ways of organising a school. Discussion of curriculum
content and values was no longer needed, when the only thing that
mattered was comparative effectiveness.

Exchange value dominates over *use value* in a régime where only
exam scores matter and not what is being learnt, and where there is
no discussion about what sort of people finally emerge from the
school.

Improvement or intensification?

School Improvement represents a fundamentally different practice
from School Effectiveness. According to David Hopkins, perhaps the
best known and most experienced British writer in this field, its key
features are:

- a bottom-up orientation in which improvement is owned by the individual school and its staff

- a qualitative methodology

- concern with changing organisational processes rather than the outcomes

- a concern to treat educational outcomes as not 'given' but problematic

- a concern to see schools as dynamic institutions requiring extended study more than 'snapshot' cross-sectional studies. (Hopkins, 2001:56)

It is the penultimate point which is most problematic. In practice, School Improvement tacitly accepts School Effectiveness's understanding of educational success. The term 'improvement' begs the question 'What do we mean by *good*?' Without debating this question, we are quite clueless about what might constitute 'better'.

Though there appears to be a certain openness when school improvement texts speak vaguely of 'outcomes' such words are invariably read in terms of the measurable outcomes acquired by politicians from effectiveness researchers. This is the inevitable default for the majority of readers living under a régime which is discursively underpinned by such keywords as 'effectiveness' and 'accountability'.

Because School Improvement pays so little attention to questions of educational purpose and social values, it inevitably collapses into a pursuit of greater efficiency, rather than a genuine attempt to rethink the purpose of schooling at a time of dramatic change.

> We have devoted such energy to developing a sophisticated knowledge of change management, planning, assessment, school cultures, leadership. Now... the question is unavoidably – *to what end, all this?* Where is the *vision*?
>
> ...Much of the high-level government interest in school improvement has led to an intensification of teaching, accountability, league tables, teachers feeling deprofessionalised and disenchanted (or leaving), a relentless drive for more though not always better – and silence on the question of *educational purpose*.

> What really matters: new targets to meet? higher maths grades
> perhaps? or caring and creative learners, a future, a sense of justice,
> the welfare of the planet and its people? (Wrigley, 2001: 1)

Though Hopkins has recently sought to open up the field in more
critical directions, his working definitions are vague. For example, in
citing Habermas' distinction between technical, practical and critical
epistemologies, and wishing to recommend the latter, he defines *critical* school improvement as 'authentic', with an emphasis on 'student
learning, intervention and empowerment', a rather vague foundation.
It is quite possible for a school staff to engage 'authentically' in a
development 'focused on learning' and which may 'empower'
students at least by increasing their self-confidence, whilst failing to
re-orientate the school towards more socially-critical aims.

Culture

One of the most positive features of the School Improvement
literature is a focus on school 'culture' as a factor in explaining and
promoting change.

> School cultures are dynamic and created through the interactions of
> people. They are a nexus of shared norms and values that express
> how people make sense of the organisation in which they work and
> the other people with whom they work. (Busher, 2001:76)

Some writers have begun to reorientate the discussion towards a
scrutiny of the dominant macropolitical assumptions:

> The culture of an organisation, then, is a construct made up of a
> range of expectations about what are proper and appropriate
> actions. This raises two very important questions... where the ex-
> pectations that define legitimate action come from and how they
> become part of the assumptive worlds of each organisational
> member. (Bennett, 2001:107-9)

In general, though, the discussion focuses too much on culture as
'capacity for change', with no attempt to clarify the kind of change
and whether it is desirable and avoids the critical questions which
might connect school culture to a discussion of context, power and
values. Within the sociological tradition, cultures are often turbulent
and contested. Understanding them requires an openness to different
perspectives, an awareness of contradictions and boundaries and conflicts of interest and ideology. There is a tendency, in School Improve-

ment's recent discovery of culture, to view culture instrumentally, as a technical means to getting certain results.

A socially critical exploration of school cultures might usefully take on board the following questions:

- what are the differences between authoritarian and cooperative cultures?

- what is the cultural significance of traditional school learning as alienated labour, i.e. students carrying out tasks because they are told to, working for set amounts of time, handing over a product which has no real purpose or audience, then receiving a token reward in the form of a mark, grade or gold star?

- how does the culture of surveillance and target setting affect learning?

- what are the cultural messages learnt by children in classrooms which are dominated by the teacher's voice and solo performance, closed questions and rituals of the transmission of superior wisdom?

- how can schools reach a better understanding of cultural difference, in order to prevent exclusion and encourage greater involvement and motivation?

- how are limiting concepts of intelligence worked out in classroom interactions – for example, intelligence as innate, or stereotypically related to social class or ethnicity?

- how do teachers' assumptions about single parents, minorities and 'dysfunctional' working-class families operate symbolically in classroom interactions? (based on Wrigley, 2003: 36-7)

The discursive practice of 'accountability' and 'leadership'

It would clearly be a mistake to treat Effectiveness and Improvement simply as *discourse* located in particular academic paradigms. Particularly in England, they form part of a totalising *discursive practice* in which:

- the goals of schooling are determined by the state-imposed National Curriculum

- an approved pedagogy is increasingly state-imposed

- normative professional roles and actions for teachers and school managers are regulated by 'Standards', competences and performance-related pay

- transgression is policed by Ofsted, which, if not quite from cradle to grave, has power over all ages from toddlers in childcare to Directors of Education

- any failure to reach government-imposed targets, however unrealistic, is stigmatised as 'ineffective' teaching or leadership

The ruthless determination to establish a seamless and total system is illustrated by the DfES handling of the Hay McBer 'research' they commissioned in support of performance pay for teachers in schools. This study simply eliminated cases where good progress resulted from teaching which did not fit the approved model. In fact, there was only a random connection between particularly good progress (even on the narrow measures used) and the approved styles of teaching. Nevertheless these teaching styles were officially adopted by the DfES as the basis for teachers' 'threshold' payments. (BERA, 2001:5-9)

Education is dominated by the ubiquitous concept of 'accountability', though no one is quite sure to whom the schools are accountable. In the absence of an audience, the concept is implicitly authoritarian, and accountability becomes a distortion of a genuine sense of *responsibility*.

> 'Accountability' is, after all, not the same thing as responsibility, still less duty. It is a pistol loaded with blame to be fired at the heads of those who cannot answer charges. (Inglis, 2000:424)

The state, as if it were a neutral and representative body which acted fairly in everyone's interests, stands proxy for any genuine relationship between partners in education: teachers, students, parents. Despite the dangers in self-policing, we can see new forms of school self-evaluation as a form of resistance. In one challenging example, the Student Voice project, school students were invited to define and carry out research projects about their own schools as a stimulus and starting point for school development planning.

The impact of the surveillance régime is manifest at many levels. Michael Fielding writes of its impact on professional values and relationships with children:

> How many teachers... are now able to listen openly, attentively, and in a non-instrumental, exploratory way to their children / students without feeling guilty, stressed or vaguely uncomfortable about the absence of criteria or the insistence of a target tugging at their sleeves. (Fielding, 1999:280)

It is resulting in subtle but crushing changes in the ways in which teachers speak about young children's learning: everything is geared towards accelerating growth against pre-specified targets within assumed norms. Accountability involves not only being constantly in view, it also amounts to a new way of *looking*. We are living through the establishment of a *virtual* panopticon.

Anyone who does not conform with this régime is labelled and discarded. For example, children, from a very early age, are being classified as 'ADHD' or 'Aspergers' if their behaviour does not conform to the classroom norms. These two labels represent opposite ends of a spectrum of non-conformity, the hyperactive and the withdrawn, alternative forms of maladjustment to the passive, decontextualised and authoritarian norms of classroom organisation and learning.

This discursive environment naturally impacts on understandings and practices of 'leadership'. Despite a growing understanding of the value of 'distributed leadership', linear models of school change predominate within hierarchies of control. The promised liberation from local government bureaucracy, as management responsibilities were shifted downwards, has turned into increasingly close supervision and diminishing opportunities for local initiative. Helen Gunter rightly describes headship in England as a form of 'middle management', since the real agenda is set elsewhere. The distribution of leadership is largely mythical:

> Shared leadership is functionally downwards. It is about getting teaching and learning done, measured and made visible in externally determined ways. Middle management [is] responsibility shifted down the line within the school. (Gunter, 2001: 111, summarising Grace, 1995)

Increasingly the neo-Taylorist approach to getting new tasks done efficiently and effectively has been given a new-wave gloss in which delegation is the means through which individuals in teams can learn and develop. (Gunter, 2001:131)

Slippages, silences, a 'selective tradition'

As a literature student, and well before poststructuralism arrived on the scene, I was excited by Raymond Williams' identification of significant textual silences and omissions. Why is it, for example, that Jane Austen uses the term 'neighbour' not to refer to the nearest human beings but to people with a suitably elevated social status? Why did Dickens resort to the magical discovery of a distant relative as a means of rescuing children from poverty? Such deconstruction, I believe, owes more to the reader's political position and understanding than a sophisticated set of deconstructive procedures.

It is equally possible to look for such textual slippages and silences in the School Improvement literature. We might ask, for instance, why writers who promise to address the specific characteristics of schools serving areas of poverty so quickly neglect their promise of focusing on 'context' and quietly substitute the concept of 'capacity for change' (as, for example, Hopkins, 2001). Books which promise to examine the historical context for the rise of School Improvement invariably censor difficult political issues such as the creation of a competitive educational market under Thatcher, the strengthening of the surveillance régime by New Labour, accelerating privatisation, and so on. Where these difficulties are mentioned, they appear in an introductory chapter, and the rest of the book is written as if they were of little importance. This removal of history and politics effectively conceals the reasons for the paradigm's dominance.

Key concepts in the texts are depoliticised by silencing the connections with social class and other forms of inequality. Thus, 'raising expectations' is seen in terms of a vaguely moralistic exhortation to children, rather than a political/cultural challenge to structures of inequality. It is a magical move which teachers are somehow expected to perform regardless of the denigration of their schools as 'failing' and the social chaos created by chronic poverty.

Perhaps the most significant absence of all is the enormous gap in the research: the relative neglect of schools in areas of poverty, whether with multi-ethnic or mainly white populations. The few books which do exist are rarely cited in the 'mainstream' School Improvement literature. Similarly, schools serving poor areas are virtually absent in Teddlie and Reynolds' *International Handbook of School Effectiveness Research* (2000); this 400-page volume includes only two or three references, selected to support a view that such schools simply need stricter discipline and a back to basics curriculum. Since substantial texts exist which support more liberating conclusions (see for example Cummins, 2000:247; Knapp *et al*, 1995; Wrigley, 2000), we are clearly dealing with a 'selective tradition', in Raymond Williams' words (1977:115). This neglect is all the more alarming given the extent of poverty in Britain, a third of school children in Scotland, half in inner London, and the manifest inability of the dominant model of School Improvement to make an impact on achievement in areas of deprivation.

Above all else, there is a deafening silence about educational aims and social values, which has a distorting effect on the entire literature. How else can we explain why books about leadership so rarely focus on *finding direction* in unknown territory, surely a prime aspect of leadership!

Blair's neo-liberal government is well served by the technical rationalism of these discursive practices by which schools are governed. The dominant version of school improvement, actively favoured through multiple forms of government sponsorship, is anti-democratic in its impact on educational change, including:

- a growing attainment gap

- the accountability and surveillance régime and culture, for teachers and students alike

- limited space for responsiveness and creativity, particularly in challenging circumstances

- teacher demoralisation and shortages, disproportionately affecting inner city schools

- the drive towards more transmission teaching

- a curriculum which limits the possibility for social understanding

A new world is possible

Alternative models of educational change are possible, in which an understanding of change processes and school cultures is reconnected with a discussion of educational and social values. (See for example the range of topics dealt with in Hargreaves *et al* 1998 and Altrichter *et al*, 1998). In a more integrated way, my own book, *Schools of Hope – a New Agenda for School Improvement* (2003), highlights the potential contribution of diverse literatures on curriculum studies, constructs of ability and intelligence, community education and social justice, which are normally neglected in the mainstream School Improvement texts.

Spaces of academic resistance can be found in the support of particular publishers and journals. We cannot however succeed at an intellectual level alone but urgently need to establish a practical alliance, uniting activists within teacher unions and subject associations such as NATE (National Association of Teachers of English) as well as organisations promoting the education of ethnic minority children and refugees and community educators. A good model for this kind of alliance can be found in the American teachers' cooperative *Rethinking Schools* whose publications both challenge government policy and share inspiring examples of critical pedagogy.

A phenomenon such as Effectiveness-based Improvement can only be understood seriously when we look at how closely its dominant tropes map onto those of capitalist society in general:

- the myth that all schools are individually capable of high levels of success, regardless of systemic inequality, if only they are properly led, echoes the Victorian 'self-made man': that rare specimen of the entrepreneur who makes his way from rags to riches through his own efforts

- learning as the 'banking' of knowledge (Freire, 1970:59), to be quantified and accounted for, and where the producers of knowledge are constantly monitored against how much they have 'added value'

- the concept of curriculum as externally imposed and fixed, just as the industrial worker receives instructions to produce goods to a set design for distant customers

- the learner's sense of reward as extrinsic to the task, and the concept that activities find their meaning separate from the emotions, creativity and personal meaning-making of the worker

- learning seen as exchange value divorced from use value, as with manufacture once finance capitalism dominates over industrial capitalism

- the school leader as site manager, an accountable agent within a project which is determined by powerful forces higher up the chain of command

Similarly, we cannot bring about a change of direction in isolation from a wider movement to transform society. We are living through a period of unbridled arrogance at the very heart of the American Empire and finally unleashed in its 'liberation' of Iraq. This has led to rejection and resistance of imperialism on a scale unprecedented in human history, symbolised by worldwide anti-war demonstrations involving over ten million people on 15 February 2003, divisions between European governments and an awakening of the Middle East. Intellectually and organisationally, diverse threads are being traced to a centre which it had become unfashionable to name: the roots of global warming, warfare, starvation in Africa and many more troubles are rightfully located in the power structures of globalising capitalism.

Poststructuralism might offer us a range of insights and techniques, but none that we can usefully deploy unless we look for coherent explanations linking educational governance with wider power structures. It would be truly ironic if, at a time of widespread political reconnection, resistance to the neo-liberal domination of education were to be dissipated by a return to the textual games and ephemeral interests of a discredited intellectual movement. Educational research as the last refuge of postmodernism? This would be tragic, not ludic. Such an abdication of responsibility is no laughing matter.

References

Altrichter H, Schley W and Schratz, M (1998) *Handbuch zur Schulentwicklung.* [Handbook of school development] Innsbruck: StudienVerlag

Angus, L (1993) The sociology of school effectiveness, in: *British Journal of Sociology of Education,* 14(3)

Bennett, N (2001) Power, structure and culture: an organisational view of school effectiveness and school improvement, in: Harris, A, and Bennett, N (eds) *School effectiveness and school improvement: alternative perspectives*. London: Continuum

BERA (2001) Report on methodological seminar on Hay/McBer enquiry into teacher effectiveness: 9 May 2001, in: *Research Intelligence*, 76

Büeler, X (1998) Schulqualität und Schulwirksamkeit, in: Altrichter, H. *et al* (eds) *Handbuch zur Schulentwicklung*. Innsbruck: StudienVerlag

Busher, H (2001) The micro-politics of change, improvement and effectiveness in schools, in: Harris, A and Bennett, N (eds) *School effectiveness and school improvement: alternative perspectives*. London: Continuum

Coleman, J S *et al* (1966) *Equality of educational opportunity*. Washington DC: Government Printing Office

Cummins, J (2000) *Language, power and pedagogy: bilingual children in the crossfire*. Clevedon: Multilingual Matters

Dickens, C (1854) *Hard Times*.

Eagleton, T (1996) *The illusions of postmodernism*. Oxford: Blackwell

Fielding, M (1999) Target setting, policy pathology and student perspectives: learning to labour in new times, in: *Cambridge Journal of Education*, 29(2)

Freire, P (1970) *Pedagogy of the oppressed*. New York: Continuum

Gunter, H (2001) *Leaders and leadership in education*. London: Chapman

Hargreaves, A, Lieberman, A, Fullan, M and Hopkins, D (eds) (1998) *International handbook of educational change*. Dordrecht: Kluwer

Hopkins, D (2001) *School improvement for real*. London: RoutledgeFalmer

Inglis, F (2000) A malediction on management, in: *Journal of Educational Policy*, 15(4)

Knapp, M, Shields, P and Turnbull, B (1995) Academic challenge in high-poverty classrooms, in: *Phi Delta Kappan*, 76(10)

OfSTED (2000) *Improving city schools*. London: HMSO www.ofsted.gov.uk

Slee, R (1998) High reliability organisations and liability students – the politics of recognition, in: Slee, R and Weiner, G with Tomlinson, S (eds) *School effectiveness for whom? Challenges to the school effectiveness and school improvement movements*. London: Falmer

Teddlie, C and Reynolds, D (2001) Countering the critics: responses to recent criticisms of school effectiveness research, in: *School Effectiveness and School Improvement*, 12(1)

Teddlie, C and Reynolds, D (2000) *International handbook of school effectiveness research*. London: RoutledgeFalmer

Williams, R (1977) *Marxism and literature*. Oxford: Oxford University Press

Wrigley, T (2000) *The power to learn – stories of success in the education of Asian and other bilingual pupils*. Stoke on Trent: Trentham

Wrigley, T (2001) Editorial, in: *Improving Schools*, 4(3)

Wrigley, T (2003) *Schools of hope – a new agenda for school improvement*. Stoke on Trent: Trentham

PART TWO
CULTURAL CONFLICT

4

Sexualities and resistance: queer(y)ing identity and discourse in education

ELIZABETH ATKINSON

While Apple's opening chapter in the first section of this book focused on cultural and moral normalisation and the fear of 'polluting' counter-cultures in education, Elizabeth Atkinson's chapter opens this second section with a focus on one specific counter-culture: that of sexuality. She argues that the sort of sexual anonymity that is demanded within educational environments contrasts markedly with the realities of teachers' and learners' lives, and suggests that in wanting to protect our children, we have promoted the 'normalisation of nothingness', while at the same time turning a blind eye both to the sexualised discourses at work in children's lives, and to their pervasive and sometimes violent effects. Atkinson suggests that the recognition of sexualities and sexual identities constitute a valid and valuable form of resistance to the normalising discourses which constitute an often implicit, and sometimes explicit, part of the grammar of teaching and learning.

Introduction

Where do you start when you start with silence? In spite of the growing literature in queer theory, the long history of gender studies as a subject in its own right and the increasing recognition of heteronormative forces in educational contexts by a small but significant body of educational researchers, there is a deafening silence on sexualities in education. The sort of sexual anonymity demanded of teachers and researchers within all phases of education is representative of a wider silencing, or neutralising, of identity for those involved in the teaching profession, which contrasts oddly with the discourses of sexuality embedded in the interactions of children and young people within and beyond the context of schooling. While colleagues in sociology, cultural studies and psychology continue a long tradition of both teaching and researching sexuality, those of us who are 'inside' education, and particularly those involved in working with teachers and children, find that attempts to address these issues within our own field are met with anxious questions, raised eyebrows or rib-nudging jokes, along with an assumption that research and teaching in this area can only be a sort of personal flag-waving that has little to do with serious academic study. This paper aims to offer a recognition of sexualities as a form of resistance to these assumptions and as a way of developing a significant but under-recognised dimension of what bell hooks (1994) describes as 'education as the practice of freedom'.

On writing, toothache, trains and sexuality

I planned this paper on a train, and wrote it with a toothache. Why is this relevant to a paper on sexualities and resistance? There are three reasons. The first is my dilemma over whether or not to take *Schooling Sexualities* (Epstein and Johnson, 1998) to read in the dentist's waiting room. After a tussle between pride and fear, I stuffed it into a bag and rehearsed my answers to curious questions all the way to the dentist's surgery, where it remained safely hidden for the duration of my visit. The second is the insult, 'Faggot', shouted by young man to the bartender as he came into my carriage on the recent rail journey during which I was planning this chapter, and my subsequent public defence of the bartender's right to complain: my first public involvement in a homophobic incident. Together, these two snapshots present two of the key reasons, silence and stigma, why we need to insist that sexualities become a site of open inquiry in education. The third reason is the very fact that this sort of intrusion of the private into the public arena, my reference to my own experiences, especially if they concern intimate or personal events, is seen as inappropriate, excessive, and indulgent.

As Debbie Epstein (1994) points out, it is exactly this refusal to cross the boundary between public and private life that maintains and perpetuates the status of sexuality in education as silent and silenced. Liz Kelly (1992) states that this public-private divide has been maintained by the distinction between an authoritarian political stance in relation to *social policy* – that is, private life as constructed by authoritarian populism – and the emphasis on freedom of choice in the *economic sphere* – that is, public life as constructed by economic liberalism. And it is by maintaining this public-private divide, by reinforcing these secrets and signs hidden behind silences, that we allow ourselves to keep up the pretence of the *absence* of sexuality in education, while its embodiment in the day-to-day educational experience of ourselves and our students impacts on everything we do. As Kelly puts it:

> sexuality in the late twentieth century [and, I would add, the early twenty-first] is both visible yet invisible, spoken about yet silenced, designated as private yet pervasively public (1992:26-27)

I could go on. I could cite the warning of a colleague that my focus on sexuality in a paper to be presented at a British Educational Research Association conference would attract unwanted press attention; the nudges and winks received by another colleague in response to her announcement of a research focus on sexuality and sex education; the statement from an anxious headteacher, when approached about researching attitudes in his school towards gay, lesbian and bisexual students, that 'It's like asking about wife battering'; the nervous and excited *frisson* that ran through my group of fifty final year Early Childhood Studies undergraduates when I showed them the gay kiss between two teenage boys in *Beautiful Thing* (Channel Four Corporation, 1996), one of the few British films in existence (outside the field of pornography) which portrays a same-sex romance between teenagers.

But why is it that if we choose, as educators, whether in schools, colleges or universities, to resist the silence, we are branded as having an unnatural and inappropriate interest in issues beyond the realm of propriety? Don't just take my word that it happens: here's the word of the President of the Midwest Sociological Society, Joane Nagel:

> The study of sexuality has been a stigmatised one in sociology and elsewhere. In the past two years that I have been working in this area, I have been challenged and heard skeptical comments from a

number of colleagues about my research, comments whose text and subtext questioned my motives, my sexuality, and the value of my work on such a 'frivolous' topic, one so marginal to the 'important' problems with which sociology should be grappling. (2000:13)

And if it is so 'frivolous' and 'unimportant', why is it that it pervades every area of educational life? 'Gender' has become such a respectable area of inquiry that the key figures of second wave feminism find themselves at the core of university reading lists across a host of disciplines whilst sexualities remain silenced, marginalised and taboo, supported by repeated moral panics fuelled in recent years in the UK, first by the Conservative backlash in the 1980s and early 1990s against the 'Loony Left' (Jones and Mahony, 1989; Epstein, 1994; Smith, 1994) and then by the determination of New Labour to appeal to a wide spectrum of the electorate to endorse its centrist policies.

Sites of education; sites of sexuality

As Epstein and Johnson state in the introduction to *Schooling Sexualities* (1998:2):

> As places of every-day-life activity as well as public or state institutions, schools are sites where sexual and other identities are developed, practiced and actively produced. Pupils, but also teachers and to a lesser extent other participants (parents, usually mothers, and other carers for example), are 'schooled' there, as gendered and sexual beings. Sexual and other social identities, as possible ways of living, are produced in relation to the cultural repertoires and institutional conditions of schooling.

Kelly echoes this view (1992:27):

> Whatever conservative ideologues might say, schools are places where sex talk, sexual behaviour, sexual relationships, sexual abuse and harassment, sexual identity, sexual divisions and sexual politics are threaded throughout the warp and weft of interactions between students, staff and students and staff. This reality exists alongside the cautious inclusion or the deliberate exclusion of sexuality in the formal taught curriculum.

This silencing of sexualities is, of course, social and political as well as anti-educational. Epstein and Johnson draw a link between concepts of sexuality and concepts of nationhood, whereby only that form of sexuality which is normalised and accepted both within and

Elizabeth Atkinson

beyond educational settings, constitutes legitimate 'Englishness'. The links between notions of 'race' and notions of sexuality are also explored by Anna Marie Smith (1994), Joane Nagel (2000) and bell hooks (1989). Epstein and Johnson identify the ways in which this sort of construction of nationhood extends beyond boundaries of race, to the exclusion of any sort of sexuality which does not meet the heterosexual norm, while Epstein, O'Flynn and Telford (2003) explore the naturalisation of heterosexuality and the silencing of transgressive sexualities from the early years to post-compulsory educational settings. The lesson to be learnt from all these studies is that by continuing to close our eyes to the implicit sexualities embedded in the formal and informal processes of schooling, and by maintaining silence in relation to sexualities in educational research, we contribute to the perpetuation of dominant discourses of sexuality. This not only denies significant aspects of teachers' and learners' identities, but leads to very real physical risks for those whose sexual identity, however silenced, is perceived as transgressive (see, for example, Trenchard and Warren, 1984; Mason and Palmer, 1996).

There is nothing new, of course, about researchers' concern over the hegemony of specific sexual norms. In 1989, for example, Carol Jones and Pat Mahony brought together accounts of the embodied nature of schooling and of the promotion of specific forms of sexuality within educational contexts, and expressed their concern (p.ix) that schools and education authorities fail to recognise 'the links between equal opportunities (gender) and issues of sexuality', and between certain forms of hegemonic masculinity and sexual violence. They make a clear link between the state's control of sexuality through education and the social control of women and girls, through what they describe as 'a highly laundered and mythologised version of heterosexuality' (p.xii). In a more recent study, Mac an Ghaill (1994) identifies the carefully restricted boundaries of masculinity through which boys learn to be men in the context of schooling.

Francis and Skelton (2001:10) identify 'the problematics of heterosexual discourses for heterosexual students and teachers' as a current and contentious issue in schooling. This goes beyond issues of sexism and sexual oppression, to the recognition, or lack of recognition, of the presence of sexuality within the processes of education, particularly in relation to motivation and passion for teaching and learning. We are not only dealing with discourses of oppression here, then, but also with discourses of *desire*.

Normalisation and resistance

The conflation of gender, sex and desire within the heterosexual matrix (Butler, 1999) renders *all* gendered behaviours in educational sites sexual, whether implicitly or explicitly. And the 'heterosexual assumption' (Foucault, 1979; Weeks *et al.*, 2001) leads to the construction of heterosexuality as a cultural norm, carrying its opposite, deviance, like a shadow:

> normalcy becomes produced and sexualised as heterosexuality, that is ... normalcy becomes inserted into sex ... the term 'heteronormativity' begins to get at how the production of deviancy is intimately tied to the very possibility of normalcy' (Britzman, 1995)

This is not, of course, unique to schooling. As Valerie Walkerdine's analysis of the sexualisation of young girls in popular culture shows (1997), classed and sexualised notions of childhood, and specifically girlhood, are deeply embedded in the representations of media and popular culture, and contribute to the maintenance of certain forms of masculinity through their opposition to a subordinate femininity. Drawing on Foucault (1979), Weeks, Heaphy and Donovan (2001) state: 'the apparatus of sexuality lies at the heart of the workings of power in modernity, and the heterosexual assumption, based on a binarism of domination and submission, is central to this.' Mac an Ghaill (1994), drawing on the work of Wolpe (1988), emphasises the fluidity and complexity of this productive process, and argues that gender and sexualities are constructed, reconstructed and negotiated in specific sites and in response to specific circumstances. They are also constructed against, and with, a range of other discourses, both public and private, a point I have explored myself elsewhere (Atkinson, 2001). And if gender and sexualities are constructed in, through, against and with discourses, then they can be turned back against those discourses as forms of resistance.

Part of this resistance might lie in a greater recognition of sexual boundary crossing, whereby marginalised and transgressive sexualities might be re-stated as productive and powerful rather than destructive and threatening. Judith Butler explores this idea of boundary crossing in relation to the work of Mary Douglas (1969):

> Douglas suggests that all social systems are vulnerable at their margins, and that all margins are accordingly considered dangerous. If the body is synecdochal for the social system per se or a site in which open systems converge, then any kind of unregulated permeability constitutes a site of pollution and endangerment. (Butler, 1999: 168)

Pillow quotes a school administrator she interviewed in the course of her research on teen pregnancy as stating, 'Bodies are dangerous' (2003: 145). A greater awareness of how boundaries are inscribed on and in bodies in educational settings, coupled with a desire to question and interrogate sexualised norms, might open up a whole new field in the realm of what Andy Sparkes (1996) calls 'body projects'.

Interrupted body projects and flexible narratives of the self

What I would like to suggest, drawing on the work of Sparkes, is that what we are experiencing in education, both through silenced sexualities and through the dominance of normalising forces, is the continuing effect of a series of 'interrupted body projects'. This means that attempts to create, negotiate or validate our sexual identity come up against barriers which constrain and limit us, and which reduce our capacities as teachers and learners. While Sparkes focuses on teachers whose identity has been interrupted by bodily injury or the prospect of decreasing fitness, I would like to broaden this concept of 'body projects' to embrace the wider field of teachers and learners in general. We are *all* experiencing 'interrupted body projects', by virtue of being involved in education.

Sparkes' analysis (1996: 181) identifies the way in which the absence of a range of narratives from which teachers might choose to represent their bodily identity leads to the construction of *disciplined* and *docile* bodies that, according to Frank (1991), become predictable through their regimentation. He goes on to state:

> there is a constant need for identities to be reflexively created, re-created and sustained by the individual through flexible narratives of the self. (Sparkes, 1996:184)

Sparkes' concern, however, is that these flexible narratives are not available to those working in educational contexts, and that there is an urgent need to interrogate this silence:

61

This would necessitate a consideration of the manner in which body stories operate to serve both conservative functions that maintain the dominant order, and also how they might have the potential to act as sites of resistance so as to transform individual lives and cultures within teaching. (1996:186)

Body projects in educational settings

While the sexual identities of teachers, particularly female teachers, and researchers, have been neutralised in educational contexts, a rash of recent significant research has demonstrated the *sexualised* nature of the gendered exchanges between pupils and pupils, and between pupils and teachers (Mac an Ghaill, 1994; Epstein, 1997; Kehily and Nayak, 1997; Epstein and Johnson, 1998; Renold, 1999, 2000; Francis and Skelton, 2001; Halstead and Waite, 2001; Reay, 2001; Atkinson, 2002; Renold, 2002).

This recent research literature abounds with telling examples. To cite just a few, Diane Reay (2001) describes how the children in her study made a clear distinction between 'girlies', 'heavily involved in gender work which even at the age of seven inscribed traditional heterosexual relations' and therefore made them legitimate targets of sexual harassment and 'nice girls', hard-working, well-behaved and therefore, as traitors to the heterosexual norm, constructed by some of the boys as 'a polluting, contagious 'other'' (p159). Emma Renold (2000) describes the preoccupation of the ten-to-eleven year old girls in her study with physical appearance, and the difficulties they had in negotiating a public identity that was 'tarty, but not too tarty' (p313); and Kehily and Nayak (1997), researching the role of humour in the production of heterosexual hierarchies among teenagers, describe the way in which 'young women and subordinate males can be seen as targets for comic displays which frequently blur the boundaries between humour and harassment' (p81). A particularly interesting dimension of this research is what it reveals about the differential status of male and female sexualities for adults in schools. While Epstein and Johnson (1998), for example, highlight the invisibility and neutralisation of women teachers through specified codes of dress and behaviour, the work of Skelton (2001), Francis and Skelton (2001) and Swain (2000; 2002) shows how visibly sexualised masculinities play a major part in the gendered behaviour of both male teachers and male pupils in primary schools.

A significant body of research has linked the dominance of particular forms of hegemonic masculinity within educational settings to sexual violence, linking Jones and Mahony's collection of women's narratives (1989) to more recent explorations of the violent discourses of children and young people in school, especially boys (see, for example, Kehily and Nayak, 1997; Halstead and Waite, 2001). As Swain puts it, (2000:96): 'Although '[hegemonic masculinity] does not necessarily involve physical violence, it is often underwritten by the threat of violence'. This is echoed in the work of Halstead and Waite (2001), who identify the way in which sexual violence forms a theme in boys' sexualised joking in the context of sex education lessons. While Halstead and Waite recognise the use of humour as a defence mechanism among these boys, they are also aware of the darker undertones of these violent discourses and their relationship to certain dominant forms of heterosexuality.

Kelly states (1992:37):

> Each time it is raised, just what this so called 'natural' family and 'normal' sexuality consists of must be highlighted: supporting 'traditional values' means supporting, rather than challenging, the existence of child sexual abuse, domestic violence, rape, sexual assault and sexual harassment. We need approaches to sexuality in education that enable children and young people [and teachers and researchers] to question, rather than accept, these realities.

Embodied learners and leaky bodies

Ironically, where sex and sexuality *have* been made the explicit focus of government policy and/or classroom teaching, the aim has been largely to reduce the effects of what has been perceived as premature sexual activity, with the specific objective of reducing teenage pregnancy figures. As Kelly puts it (1992:32–33, drawing on (Lenskyj, 1990): 'The implicit message in the traditional 'plumbing and prevention' approach is that it is girls' knowledge and activity which is both the problem and the target'. This objective has tended to obscure wider aims for a broadening of sexuality education, although there is the beginning of a recognition, embedded in the Department for Education and Employment guidelines on Sex and Relationship Education (DfEE, 2000) of the need to support and reflect young people's developing sexual identity, whatever form it might take. In contrast to this liberal approach, the neutralising of young women's and men's sexual bodies within the school environment, through the silencing of discourses of sexuality and desire, denies their sexual maturity, and is deeply embedded within discourses of class and power. Pillow reminds us of this (1997; 2003) when she considers the classed nature of state teen pregnancy programmes, in which girls identified as having low socio-economic status are constructed as having 'made mistakes' and as needing to demonstrate their potential for responsible behaviour to school and society. In the context of these programmes, sexual activity is perceived as lower-class, and not something in which middle-class girls are expected to indulge. This assumption plays a significant part in the way in which teenage girls choose to use their bodies as sites of resistance (Pillow, 1997; Hey, 1997; Epstein and Johnson, 1998).

Sexualities and resistance: queer(y)ing identity and discourse in education

Nagel (2000:3) draws our attention to the 'sometimes conspicuous, sometime concealed ways in which sexuality underpins the logic of social life, political policies, and personal and public political decisions' and suggests that the interrogation of sexuality as 'the intimate substructure of social life' (p2) offers 'the same promise that unveiling gender did a generation ago – the promise to reveal to us our own presumptions and prejudices and to allow us to think the unthinkable' (p3). Similarly, Leslie Bloom (1999:331) states: 'interpreting sexuality must be as salient to educational qualitative research as interpreting gender, race, and ethnicity have become'.

As Butler (1999) and hooks (1994) remind us, harnessing sexuality as a site of resistance challenges the Cartesian dualism which for centuries has rationalised the separation of mind and body. As hooks puts it (1994:192):

> Entering the classroom determined to erase the body and give ourselves over more fully to the mind, we show by our beings how deeply we have accepted the assumption that passion has no place in the classroom.

I have suggested that the recognition of sexualities and sexual identities constitutes a valid and valuable form of resistance to the normalisation of identity which constitutes an often implicit, and sometimes explicit, part of the grammar of teaching and learning. In seeking to promote a safe and neutral environment for the promotion of learning, we have generated an educational world in which real, embodied selves have little place. In doing so, we have sanctioned and institutionalised the normalisation of nothingness, the assumption that those who teach are not actually people at all, and that those who learn can only resume their full identities once they leave the classroom. At the same time, we turn a blind eye to the explicit sexualisation of young children's identity, especially that of girls, through fashion, toys and popular culture and to the ways in which this affects the development and reinforcement of specific bounded, sexed and gendered identities from the earliest years of schooling.

I would like to suggest, however, that queer(y)ing identity and discourse in education allows us to achieve three possibilities: 1) a recognition that sexuality – and its place in education – is deeply political; 2) a refusal to erase the body in conducting education as the practice of freedom; and 3) a resistance to the unquestioned dominance of often oppressive sexual norms.

There is hope for the future.

Elizabeth Atkinson is the Convenor of the Sexualities Special Interest Group in the British Educational Research Association.

References

Atkinson, E (2001) Deconstructing boundaries: out on the inside?, in: *International Journal of Qualitative Studies in Education*, 14(3): 307-316

Atkinson, E (2002) Education for diversity in a multisexual society: negotiating the contradictions of contemporary discourse, in: *Sex Education*, 2(2): 119-132

Bloom, L R (1999) Interpreting interpretation: gender, sexuality and the practice of not reading straight, in: *International Journal of Qualitative Studies in Education*, 12(4): 331-345

Britzman, D (1995) Is there a queer pedagogy? Or stop reading straight, in: *Educational Theory*, 45: 151-165

Butler, J (1999) *Gender Trouble. Feminism and the subversion of identity* (tenth anniversary edition). London: Routledge

Department for Education and Employment (DFEE) (2000) *Sex and Relationship Education Guidance. DfEE ref. 0116/2000*. London: Department for Education and Employment

Douglas, M (1969) *Purity and Danger*. London: Routledge and Kegan Paul

Epstein, D (1994) Introduction: Lesbian and gay equality in education – problems and possibilities, in: Epstein, D (ed) *Challenging Lesbian and Gay Inequalities in Education*. Buckingham: Open University Press

Epstein, D (1997) Boyz' Own Stories: masculinities and sexualities in schools, in: *Gender and Education*, 9(1): 105-115

Epstein, D and Johnson, R (1998) *Schooling Sexualities*. Buckingham: Open University Press

Epstein, D, O'Flynn, S and Telford, D (2003) *Silenced Sexualities in Schools and Universities*. Stoke-on-Trent: Trentham Books

Foucault, M (1979) *The History of Sexuality. Volume 1: an introduction*. Harmondsworth: Penguin

Francis, B and Skelton, C (2001) Men teachers and the construction of hetero-sexual masculinity in the classroom, in: *Sex Education*, 1(1): 9-21

Frank, A (1991) For a sociology of the body: an analytical review, in: Feather-stone, M, Hepworth, M and Turner, B (eds) *The Body*. London: Sage

Halstead, J M and Waite, S (2001) 'Living in different worlds': gender differences in the developing sexual values and attitudes of primary school children, in: *Sex Education*, 1(1): 59-76

Hey, V (1997) *The Company She Keeps: An ethnography of girls' friendship*. Buckingham: Open University Press

hooks, b (1989) *Talking Back – Talking Feminist, Talking Black*. London: Sheba

hooks, b (1994) *Teaching to Transgress: Education as the practice of freedom*. London: Routledge

Jones, C and Mahony, P (eds) (1989) *Learning Our Lines: Sexuality and social control in education*. London: The Women's Press

Kehily, M J and Nayak, A (1997) 'Lads and laughter': humour and the production of heterosexual identities, in: *Gender and Education*, 9(1): 69-87

Kelly, L (1992) Not in front of the children: responding to right wing agendas on sexuality and education, in: Arnot, M and Barton, L (eds) *Voicing Concerns: Sociological perspectives on contemporary education reforms*. Wallingford: Triangle Books, 20-40

Lenskyj, H (1990) Beyond plumbing and prevention: feminist approaches to sex education, in: *Gender and Education*, 2: 217-230

Mac an Ghaill, M (1994) *The Making of Men: Masculinities, sexualities and schooling*. Buckingham: Open University Press

Mason, A. and Palmer, A (1996) *Queer Bashing: A national survey of hate crimes against lesbians and gay men*. London: Stonewall

Nagel, J (2000) Sexualising the sociological: queering and queerying the intimate substructure of social life. Presidential address to the Midwest Sociological Society, in: *The Sociological Quarterly*, 41(1): 1-17

Pillow, W (1997) Exposed methodology: the body as a deconstructive practice, in: *International Journal of Qualitative Studies in Education*, 10(3): 349-363

Pillow, W (2003) 'Bodies are dangerous': using feminist genealogy as policy studies methodology, in: *Journal of Education Policy*, 18(2): 145-159

Reay, D (2001) 'Spice Girls', 'Nice Girls', 'Girlies', and Tomboys': gender dis-courses, girls' cultures and femininities in the primary classroom, in: *Gender and Education*, 13(2): 153-166

Renold, E (1999) Presumed Innocence: An ethnographic exploration into the construction of sexual and gender identities in the primary school. Unpublished PhD thesis. University of Wales, Cardiff

Renold, E (2000) 'Coming out': gender, (hetero)sexuality and the primary school, in: *Gender and Education*, 12(3): 309-326

Renold, E (2002) Presumed innocence: sexualised bullying and harassment in the primary school. Unpublished paper, University of Wales, Cardiff

Scheurich, J J and Young, M D (1997) Coloring epistemologies: are our research epistemologies racially biased?, in: *Educational Researcher*, 26(4): 4-16

Skelton, C (2001) *Schooling the Boys: Masculinities and primary education.* Buckingham: Open University Press

Smith, A M (1994) *New Right Discourse on Race and Sexuality. Britain, 1968-1990.* Cambridge: Cambridge University Press

Sparkes, A C (1996) Interrupted body projects and the self in teaching: exploring an absent presence, in: *International Studies in Sociology of Education*, 6(2): 167-189

Swain, J (2000) 'The money's good, the fame's good, the girls are good': the role of playground football in the construction of young boys' masculinity in a junior school, in: *British Journal of Sociology of Education*, 21(1): 95-109

Swain, J (2002) The Right Stuff: fashioning an identity through clothing in a junior school, in: *Gender and Education*, 14(1): 53-69

Trenchard, L and Warren, H (1984) *Something To Tell You.* London: London Gay Teenage Group

Walkerdine, V (1997) *Daddy's Girl: Young girls and popular culture.* London: Macmillan

Weeks, J, Heaphy, B and Donovan, C (2001) *Same Sex Intimacies: Families of choice and other life experiments.* London: Routledge

Wolpe, A M (1988) *Within School Walls: The role of discipline, sexuality and the curriculum.* London: Routledge

5

Combating cultural imperialism in Canada: a new role for adult educators?

RICHARD BOND

In this chapter, Richard Bond describes the development of an Aboriginal undergraduate degree/certificate programme, and discusses the effects it has had on indigenous communities in Canada. The larger social and political implications for Aboriginal and mainstream relationships are considered for a society in which First Nation people are emerging as survivors of attempts to assimilate them into mainstream culture. The chapter recalls Apple's analysis of cultural homogenisation and normalisation, applying this analysis specifically to a postcolonial context.

The development of an Aboriginal undergraduate degree/ certificate programme is described and the effects it has had on Aboriginal communities in Canada are discussed. Further, the constructs used to develop the Aboriginal programme provided the basis for a programme intended for non-Aboriginals. Aboriginal self-image and larger social and political implications for Aboriginal and mainstream relationships are considered for a society in which Aboriginal people are emerging as survivors of attempts to assimilate them into mainstream society.

Introduction, historical and political background

I live in Mohawk territory, as does one of our sons, his wife and children. Another one of our sons, his wife and children live in territory which once belonged to the now vanished Neutral First Nation, so called because they would ally with no other group. Tecumseh, the great Shawnee warrior and ally of the British, defeated the American invasion of the war of 1812 so that this territory could remain in British hands. Our oldest son, his wife and child live in Peyote territory. The next territory to where they live belongs to the Nez Percé. I occasionally remark that my part-Cherokee grandson in Oregon legitimises my presence in North America. There is an enduring conflict in my life resulting from the fact that I am a privileged member of the dominant cultural group in Canada. I am also a Canadian with blood links to an oppressed and dispossessed people because my grandchild's ancestors were forcibly removed from their traditional lands in what is now South Carolina and Alabama, were driven west and eventually contained on reservations in Oklahoma. Further, my privileged professional background has provided me with knowledge I would, at times, rather not have. I cannot undo the past, for what has been done is done. I cannot make it better, for the damage to the cultural history of the Aboriginal people is permanent. I *can* try to prevent worse things happening in the future. There is an old saying: *Three things come not back: The sped arrow; the spoken word; the lost opportunity.* The sped arrow and the spoken word have gone. Some opportunities have been lost, but not all. I can seize whatever opportunities are made manifest to me to work towards fostering relationships in a good way, and to try to heal.

From first serious attempts at colonisation by Europeans four hundred years ago, when early colonists learned to cooperate with and receive assistance from the Aboriginal people, Europeans have steadily assumed a mastership over the land and the people therein. The story runs that when early settlers arrived they asked for land to farm. The Aboriginals, with no concept of ownership in the same way Europeans had (Battiste, Little Bear *et al.*, 1998), and on the presumed assumption that Europeans held land in common and would simply move to a better spot when the soil and crops deteriorated, invited the settlers to help themselves, which they did. Sometimes settlers and later, serious colonisers, would offer some token in return, which the Aboriginals would accept as gifts, gift giving being part of Aboriginal culture, but did not understand that the gifts were perceived by the settlers as payment, legitimising a business transaction. This accounts for the legendary barrel of beads and assorted odds and ends given for the 'purchase' of the island of Manhattan. Land acquisition by one means or another in the United States very quickly galvanised the fledgling Canadian colony to build the great railroad west to the Pacific, thus securing a huge colony for Britain, which prevented the United States from furthering acquisitions to the north. The Aboriginal people were not simply without a voice in their own land. They were nonentities.

Two major attempts to assimilate the Aboriginal peoples of Canada into mainstream culture have had a damaging effect on that culture. The first initiative was the intense work of the European Christian missionaries, which resulted in the destruction of the potlatch, the sundance and the pow-wows. Missionaries believed totem poles to be idols and destroyed as many as they could.

The second initiative was the forced, government-assisted abduction of hundreds of thousands of Aboriginal children from their families across Canada to placement in residential schools run mainly by Roman Catholic and Anglican churches. The treatment meted out to the children has taken the form of physical and psychological abuse, as the result of efforts by church caregivers to prevent the children from speaking their native languages, participating in the cultural and religious practices and dressing in traditional attire. Even the given names of Aboriginal children have been lost and replaced by European names. There are many Aboriginals who now think white. There are others who are in a cultural limbo and psychological turmoil. Others are aware of their cultural tenets and attempt to live by the old religious and social systems now, which are badly damaged.

Beginnings of an idea and practice

The degree/certificate programme offered from the Centre for Adult Studies and Distance Learning at Brock University had its origins in 1993 when a partnership between Brock University and TVOntario was developed and the sum of $1.3 million was put together by the two partners to develop a university based multi-media delivery programme of five undergraduate courses in adult education. This initiative was made in response to requests from the Colleges of Applied Arts and Technology (CAATs) to the university to develop a programme to provide teaching credentials for CAAT instructors who do not normally have them. Such a programme would provide a second degree to CAAT faculty already in possession of a degree, or a certificate for those who had no degree. By far the largest student group was composed of CAAT instructors, with a few from business, industry and health science disciplines engaged in staff training.

Shortly after this programme was initiated and work had started on its development, an Aboriginal CAAT employee (John Hodson, 1995) drafted some ideas for a similar programme designed for Aboriginal people using their own cultural constructs. The intention was to bring into being a programme created and taught by Aboriginals for Aboriginals, which would be seen as separate from mainstream theoretical constructs and free of Eurocentric structures. It would be university-based and carry identical academic weight to mainstream programmes. North American educational programmes offered for Aboriginals have a history of lower academic standards and there is mistrust by Aboriginals of educational programmes designed and implemented for them by non-Aboriginals.

Hodson's notion was new. There are many educational programmes designed by mainstream educators and delivered to Aboriginal groups by them. (Some websites are listed in the bibliography giving access to further information about educational provision for Aboriginal Canadians.) The success rate in terms of Aboriginals obtaining educational credentials delivered by this means is poor. Programme dropout rates are high and levels of attainment are low. Reports of self-destructive behaviours among Aboriginals indicates poor individual self-image and desperation. The *Saskatchewan Indian* has reported that in the 15-24 age group, suicide is ten times higher than in the non-native populations; that alcoholism is 23% higher than among non-natives and that 48% of off-reserve families suffer from drug and alcohol abuse (October, 1988, pp. 104A-107A). Academics identify the deleterious effects of cultural hybridisation (Barman, Hébert and McCaskill, 1986; Hill, 1995; Haig-Brown, 1995; Duran and Duran, 1995; Chrisjohn and Young, 1997; Battiste, 2000; Hampton, 2000).

The programme has had a significant impact on Aboriginal education in Canada. Because of it, during the initial discussion of the desired shape and form of the up-coming revisions of the existing mainstream programme, the team, consisting of Aboriginal, French, English, Anglo-Canadian, Latvian and Estonian members, hit upon the idea of transposing some Aboriginal constructs into mainstream education.

The purpose behind this thinking was to remove or reduce Euro-centric individualistic thinking and use constructs which would be conducive to community well-being instead. These could be identified as transformational learning rather than transactional learning. Business and industry is very much focused on transactional method, servant leadership. Greenleaf (1977) asserts that true leaders are chosen by their followers and develop power through awareness, foresight and listening skills as opposed to coercion, manipulation and persuasion. Critical rather than positivistic approaches are needed to support problem solving and the elimination of top-down approaches to education and organisations.

Theoretical underpinnings

In terms of education and leadership, Apps (1994) has identified a basic need for vision making. Vision making is what led the team to view the construction of university courses for mainstream students in an atypical format, derived from the constructs of a people which, although subjugated, influence the lives of all the inhabitants of Canada, whether or not they always realise it. So the team began with the vision, which was to make something different and yet relevant; to move away from Eurocentric thinking to a mode of thinking relevant to life in Canada; to come to terms with the recognition that Europeans have colonised a land, but live with the Aboriginal inhabitants; to recognise that those of us who live here may learn from the best each society has to offer, rather than the worst; to face the fact that we, as Canadians, can learn and adapt our learning and thinking to enable us to heal relationships, build cross-cultural communities and repair the damage of four hundred years of colonisation.

Adult education has a global perspective. This is an important consideration if educators are to develop programmes designed to bridge cross-cultural boundaries. Merriam and Brockett (1997) have suggested that because adult educators serve individuals from many different countries, an international perspective is imperative. It is, of course, impossible to design programmes which would consider all aspects of individual cultures. However, all cultures have some commonalities, and it was felt that identifying the commonalities would be valuable in providing underpinnings to course development. This world view enables educators to identify contradictions in their own cultures as well as those in others, to identify the oppressors and the oppressed, and makes living with contradictions exciting and invigorating. By taking this perspective adult educators can trace the development of education from its religious origins, to modern industrial approaches and current postmodernist conditions. The combination of world view and historical perspective lends breadth and depth to this approach to adult education.

The matter of educating adults may be much more about dealing with organisations than it is with any other aspect of education because organisations are mechanisms for pursuing collective goals in societies (Scott, 1998). The origins of cultural and racial organisations are often obscure, but their current manifestations affect our lives in hundreds of subtle ways. Organisations are also about social, psychological and economic structures, which provide accounts of the behaviours of people, not only what people are doing, but what they believe they are doing and what kinds of explanations they give for their behaviour (Gray, 1988). Theoretical notions of organisations are developed from manifest human behaviours interpreted as having more than a localised, individualistic meaning. Behaviours are determined by subjective perceptions, by individual interests and by a range of existing organisational structures. From this it is possible to view educational organisations as much more than simply places where people learn facts and details. Educational organisations can be centres for social change.

Fullan (1999) has stated that theories of education and of change need each other, and that the distinction between the two is not all that clear. Good theories or programmes that are to be taken on widely must include a focus on context. In the case of the programme discussed in this chapter, the great range of cultural variables are met not in a confrontational manner but in a spirit of mutual respect for cultural difference.

Apps (1994, p.6) has argued that people are in a new time, an emerging age in which old solutions to problems and old leadership strategies do not work. Adult education organisations and their leaders need stability, but are also challenged to change. Leadership in this context may be identified in terms of the functions of leaders in adult education, in the development and implementation of adult education theories and teaching strategies, and also in the purpose of educating adults. Taken one stage further, this means training adults to be instruments of social change.

For four hundred years, the dominant culture in North America has been solidly Eurocentric, deriving from the social and political structures of Spain, France and Britain, the latter with a remarkable political and legal identity derived from England, and a pervading social influence from Scotland and Ireland. Current social change identifies forms of indigenous leadership which are emerging as valid alternatives to European models. How many people are aware that the American eagle is actually a Mohawk symbol? The clues identifying indigenous leadership constructs are all around.

Native leadership is complex. There are many Aboriginal First Nations, some of them few in population. There is great variety in leadership practices. However, they also have many common means by which they independently manage their affairs. Aboriginal theories, as with mainstream theories, develop from the behaviours of humans and over time provide the constructs within which societies are seen to thrive.

There is much dissatisfaction among Aboriginal people about the quality of education offered to their children, much of which concerns the lack of relevance to their lives and their lack of involvement in the design and implementation of the curriculum (Jules, 1990). There have been five main phases of Aboriginal education: traditional education; education by missionaries; residential schools; integrated education and, ultimately, Aboriginal control of Aboriginal education. A great deal of progress has been made in Aboriginal education over the past fifteen years. Part of this is due to the federal government's changed attitude toward Aboriginal education, part is due to the First Nations having a much greater voice than previously heard, and part is due to the increase in the numbers of Aboriginal academics.

The issue of Aboriginal versus mainstream education is a complex one, given the very great differences in terms of approaches to education. The differences may be most easily illustrated by the example of a triangle. In Aboriginal cultures, the base (the people) is on top and the apex (the leader) below. The people are supreme. In mainstream cultures, the position is reversed. An Aboriginal commentator states (Spiller *et al.*, 1984):

> What the department of Indian Affairs has imposed on us is the non-Indian version of leadership. What needs to be done is to turn the triangle around again. Rather than having a manager at the top telling people how they should go about things, we need to get back to sharing responsibility for our destiny. We need to get back to the interconnected and interrelated way of doing things.

There are many problems in the Aboriginal communities as the result of conflicting values. Most of the conflicts have arisen as the result of children being educated in non-native ways returning to the reserves. They have not been taught ways of life by their elders, and the ways they have learned from Eurocentric curricula are not suited to lives among Aboriginal people. As elders die, old ways and traditions are lost. Some remaining traditions and ways of life are irreparably damaged. Often, the result of such hybridisation is an unhappy amalgam of Aboriginal and European ways where both cultures are poorly understood.

Archibald (1984, pp 6-7) has stated

> Many educators seem to believe that Indian people did not practice an education system that possessed a credible depth of knowledge, understanding and viable educational principles ... Contrary to this view is the fact that the education systems of Indian people traditionally adopted what is known as the holistic approach ... important things such as values and higher levels of knowledge about history and environment were told through their stories and private conversations with children. The Elders also took a major responsibility in preparing the younger generation for specialised roles.

In developing the curriculum for the core courses for the Adult Education programme for Aboriginal Adult Educators, the team incorporated Aboriginal constructs as a framework for development and recognised that the holistic approach to developing a curriculum for mainstream students could easily accommodate some transcultural activity. Educators influence the education of children by educating adults, if only because of the way adults influence children's learning. As a pattern for our holistic approach the team started with the medicine wheel.

The Medicine Wheel

The Medicine Wheel is an Aboriginal symbol used to provide a framework for an holistic approach to views of the human condition. The team first used it in the development of the Aboriginal Adult Education programme, as it seemed appropriate, and in the hope that Aboriginal people would recognise that the courses were more than *white courses with feathers.*

The Medicine Wheel described here originated in the prairies in what is now known as Alberta, although all of the Aboriginal nations in Canada appear to have their equivalents by which they structure their lives. It was originally a structure designed to use as a framework for educating youngsters in various aspects of life's responsibilities. At times the physical structures were massive and of great age, incorporating huge stones as part of the design parameters. Many have been destroyed as roads were driven through them, much like Avebury in England.

The Medicine Wheel is a circle divided into quadrants, like St. Andrew's cross. However, the quadrant boundaries are not sharply defined because there is blending and overlap of the quadrant contents. The quadrants represent the great ethnic groupings of the world: white for Europeans, black for Africans, yellow for the people of the East and red for the indigenous peoples of the Americas. There is a belief among Aboriginal people that each of the races has a unique characteristic which can be shared with the others to good purpose. The quadrants are also divided into the points of the compass: the top and bottom quadrants are North (White) and South (Red) and the right and left quadrants are East (Yellow) and West (Black). Each quadrant is also associated with a sacred plant: North is cedar, South is sweetgrass, East is tobacco, and West is sage. These plants are burned individually or collectively at sacred gatherings or to promote a sense of goodness and serious intent at meetings such as pow-wows.

The quadrants further represent aspects of the human condition. North is Action and accommodates the *emotional* aspect of ourselves. South is Relationships and accommodates the *physical* aspects of ourselves. East is Vision, and accommodates the *spiritual* aspects of ourselves. West is Knowledge, and accommodates the *intellectual* aspects of ourselves. The four components offer a balanced approach to dealing with life issues, including our education, whether in teaching hands-on skills in the workforce, or in teaching intellectual skills. The attributes of the four great ethnic groups, as identified by Aboriginal people are Action (White); Vision (Yellow); Relationships (Red) and Knowledge (Black).

The use of the Medicine Wheel keeps a focus on racial differences but reminds us of our racial interdependency, our basic human qualities and our capacity for higher thought and a spiritual approach to life. The circle theme is common in Aboriginal culture. Aboriginal meetings take place in a circle so that there is no perceived order of seniority. Mainstream meetings take place at rectangular tables with the most senior person at the top and participants are arranged along the sides in order of their seniority. The sessions are led by a designated chair, or the most senior person chairs the meetings. Aboriginals speak in no particular order, but merely signal a wish to speak. There are no time limits imposed on the speaker, who holds the floor for as long as he or she holds a talking stick. When that person has finished speaking, the talking stick is passed to the next speaker and the rest of the group is silent.

A great emphasis in Aboriginal communities is a drive for community and social well being or a good state of functioning. Broadly speaking, Aboriginals learn by example because of a tradition of hands-on skill transmission. Industrialised communities are more likely learn by direction, because of the hierarchal structures of their organisations. The Medicine Wheel has been used as guide for well being in Aboriginal communities for millennia and its use in developing curriculum is seen as a means of promoting healthy communities, through educating people to help themselves and others. Its particular use is to break the cycle of dependency on government agencies, alcohol and drugs. For non-Aboriginals, it assists in the development of holistic approaches to problem solving and sensitivity to the strengths of multi-cultural endeavour. It can also work to break the cycle of dependency on alcohol and drugs with this group.

The course sample – ADED 4F07

The course title is *Understanding Organisations and Leadership in Adult Education*. Could there ever be a connection between the ancient wisdom of the Aboriginal folk and the seemingly focused

Eurocentricity of the course title? It was perceived necessary to devise a title which would appeal to a mainstream audience and at the same time allow for a content as different as possible from a recipe book approach. The Team believed it was necessary to develop a *how to think*, rather than a *how to do* course. The university requires the course to provide 78 hours of in-class or web-based, multi-media instruction and has an academic value of one undergraduate course credit. It is one of five undergraduate courses offered in Adult Education for mainstream students and five undergraduate courses offered for Aboriginal students. All courses have identical academic value.

The skills identified in the course are time management, perspective taking, developing relationships in a community of learners, listening skills, scholarly reading, scholarly writing, critical thinking, reflective practice, planning and delivering presentations, preparing instruction for adults, instructional methods, evaluation methods, case study analysis, group problem solving and dealing with conflict. The course content was designed to foster attitudes in adult learners and instructors, such as respect for self and others, respect for the process of learning, interest and understanding of learners as multi-dimensional beings, enthusiasm for learning, compassion for self and others, openness to new learning, ability to deal with failure as a learning experience, developing realistically high ideals and standards for professional practice.

Several elements of the course are directly derived from the elements identified in the Medicine Wheel. These include exercises involving sharing, trust building, considering all contributions without judgment, creating a climate of free expression, working at a friendly environment which fosters unity, openness, care, courtesy, dignity and moderation, and aiming for consensus but when this is impossible, the majority should rule.

Learners are assigned groups identified by the colours in the Medicine Wheel. Group behaviours in a given exercise are identified by the colours. Thus, the Yellow group will examine the problem from a Visionary perspective: What could be?, the Red group from the Relationship perspective: What relationships need to exist?, the Black group from the Knowledge perspective: What learning needs to take place? What information is required?, the White group from the Action perspective: What actions should be taken?

Readings in the course are not typical of what one might expect to find in a course titled Understanding Organisations and Leadership in Adult Education. The constructs identified in the Medicine Wheel are typically not found in mainstream work, nor are they tools for community building. Searching for souls and spirit (Bolman and Deal (2001), using Monet to teach leadership (Barber *et al.*, 2001), listening to other cultures (Tannen, 1998) and turning to one another: simple conversations to restore hope to the future (Wheatley, 2002), are not common mainstream approaches to understanding organisations and leadership.

Crossing cultural boundaries

Much of the content of this course, and indeed the content of all five courses, has been transported from Aboriginal culture into a mainstream culturally based university programme. This is such a departure from the North American cultural norm as to be quite revolutionary. The impact on the Aboriginal community is significant because for the first time Aboriginal culture is seen as being respected by mainstream culture, taught to non-Aboriginal students and offered at a non-Aboriginal university. It is done in a quiet, unobtrusive manner and with the aim of changing administrative, organisational and leadership practices from the current top-down models.

Healing and liberation

The process initiated by the development of this programme has gone some small way toward healing the bitter relationships which have existed between mainstream and Aboriginal communities for four hundred years. At the same time, the effort has had a liberating effect on both communities. For the Aboriginal people, the recognition of the value of the old ways, after centuries of government and church denigration, is a vindication of their past. For the mainstream community it promotes emphasis on cross-cultural community building, instead of building one community at the expense of another.

After the five original Aboriginal courses were offered, we conducted some field research to obtain a sense of how the Aboriginal communities were reacting to a web-based version of the courses. We received 534 responses, unusual for a typically reticent community. Some of the responses are as follows:

You make me proud to be Indian and proud to be learning. you must be proud of your school for letting you do this for all Indian people.

Brock, this is very substantive content and done in a very respectful way for all Aboriginals to understand. This material would be very good for health care workers to use on the Reserve. As a nurse who is studying computers, I see now how our culture can become stronger with technology if we use it properly. Thank you at Brock for helping to show us the way to use it. I will show this to my Mother and she will feel very proud that the university has understood the importance of culture and traditions.

The content made me very happy. It is everything I tell my granddaughter every day. The content was created by Indians for Indians.

This is the first time I see stuff on the computer that makes me proud to be Indian, and makes me feel people understand what it is like to be that way.

All the Aboriginal teachers here at the college are talking about this. Brock should be very proud of this site. It is the first site I have seen that is truly Indian. Thanks, Brock, for setting the example.

I am very old and am very happy my grand-daughter learns this at the college. It is good to know these machines will help to save our culture and not to ruin it.

Conclusions

The programme we have developed is intended to go way beyond the immediate. As things stand, the picture looks good. However, if the team concentrated solely on creating a few good quality courses we should not have achieved very much. The purpose of this venture is to change people's thinking and, consequently, their long-range behaviours. It is to help re-shape Canadian society.

We would not wish for Aboriginals to become like Europeans or Europeans to be like Aboriginals. Our intention has been, and continues to be, to honour our differences and to regard one another's cultures with respect, to build interdependent communities, to learn from the ancients the ways of living together without conflict and to channel our energies positively into shaping our organisations and institutions. A tall order? Not necessarily.

Acknowledgments

I am greatly indebted to the following colleagues who made the success of the programme possible. They include, in no particular order, John Hodson of the Mohawk First Nation; Janie Hodson; Tiiu Strauss; Carmen Robinson of the Lakota of the Sioux First Nation; Linda McGregor of the Métis; Denise Paquette-Frenette; Julie Dixon; members of the Odawa, Ojibway and Miqmaq First Nations, who directly and indirectly contributed so much to the programme. I am further indebted for the continuous support of the Dean of the Faculty of Education at Brock University, Michael Manley-Casimir, and the Vice-President Academic, Terry Boak. Special thanks are due to the Federal Government Office of Learning Technologies (Community Learning Networks) for a $25,000 grant to conduct a learning needs assessment.

References

Apps, J (1994) Approaches to vision making, in: Apps, J (1994) *Leadership for the emerging age: Transforming practice in adult and continuing education.* San Francisco, CA: Jossey-Bass

Archibald, J (1984) Locally developed Native studies curriculum: An historical and philosophical rationale. Paper presented at the International Conference of the Mokakit Indian Education Research Association, London, ON. July 1984

Barber, E, Chandler S and Collins, E (2001) Using Monet to teach leadership, in: *Journal of Curriculum Theorising*

Barman, J, Hébert, J, McCaskill, D (1986). *Indian education in Canada: The legacy. Vol I.* Vancouver: UBC Press

Battiste, M (2000). Foreword, in: Castellano, M, Davis, L and Lahache, L (eds) *Aboriginal education: Fulfilling the promise.* Vancouver: UBC Press

Battiste, M, Little Bear, L, *et al.* (1998) Discussion paper on indigenous knowledge and intellectual property. Unpublished

Bolman, L and Deal, T (2001) In search of soul and spirit and leaning into your fear, in: Bolman, L and Deal, T (2001) *Leading with soul.* San Francisco, CA: Jossey-Bass

Brookfield, S (2000) Transformative learning as ideology critique, in: Mezirow, J (2000) *Learning as transformation: Critical perspectives on a theory in progress.* San Francisco, CA: Jossey-Bass

Chrisjohn, R and Young, S (1997) *The circle game: Shadows and substance in the residential school experience in Canada.* Penticton BC: Theytus.

The original research report on which the book is based is available on the CD-ROM: For seven generations: An information legacy of the Royal commission on Aboriginal peoples. 1997. Ottawa: Libraxus

Cranton, P (2000) *Planning instruction for adult learners* (2nd Ed). Toronto: Wall and Emerson

Duran, E, and Duran, B (1995). *Native American postcolonial psychology.* Albany NY: SUNY Press

Fullan, M (1999) Complexity and the change process, in: Fullan, M (1999) *Change forces: The sequel.* Philadelphia, PA: Falmer Press

Gray, H (1988) A perspective on organisation theory, in: Westaby, A (ed) *Culture and power in educational organisations.* Milton Keynes, UK: Open University Press

Greenleaf, R (1977) *Servant-Leadership: A journey into the nature of legitimate power and greatness.* Mahwah, NJ: Paulist Press

Haig-Brown, C (1995) *Taking control: Power and contradiction in First Nations adult education.* Vancouver: UBC Press

Hampton, E (2000) First Nations-controlled university education in Canada, in: Castellano, M, Davis, L and Lahache, L (eds) *Aboriginal education: Fulfilling the promise.* Vancouver: UBC Press

Hill, D (1995) Aboriginal teachings as foundational principles for learning, in: *Aboriginal access to post-secondary education, PLA and Aboriginal programs of learning.* Ontario: First Nations Technical Institute and Loyalist College

Jules, F (1990) Native Indian Leadership, in: *Canadian Journal of Native Education,* 23(2): 40-56

Merriam, S and Brockett, R (1997) The global context of adult education, in: Merriam, S and Brockett, R *The profession and practice of adult education.* San Francisco CA: Jossey-Bass

Saskatchewan Indian, pp104A-107A: 1988

Selman, G *et al* (1998) *The foundations of adult education in Canada* (2nd Ed). Toronto: Thompson Educational Publishing

Scott, W (1998) Common and divergent interests, in: Scott, W *Organisations: Rational, natural and open systems* (4th Ed). Upper Saddle River, NJ: Prentice Hall

Spiller, A and Association (1984) *I am an Indian: The circle of leadership* (video).

Tannen, D (1998) What other ways are there? Listening to other cultures, in: *The argument culture.* New York NY: Viking

Wheatley, M (2002) Willing to be disturbed, in: Wheatley, M *Turning to one another: Simple conversations to restore hope to the future.* San Francisco, CA: Berrett-Koehler Publishers

Websites for further information about Aboriginal Educational provision in Canada:

Cultural/Educational Centres Program

Elementary/Secondary Education

Final Report of the Minister's National Working Group on Education – December 2002 First Nations and Inuit Youth Employment Strategy

Gathering Strength – Investing in Education Reform 1999 – 2000

Gathering Strength – Investing in Education Reform 2000 – 2001

Gathering Strength – Investing in Education Reform – Some Community Examples... Post-Secondary Education Programs

- Aboriginal Post-Secondary Education and Labour Market Outcomes Canada, 1996
- Increase in Post-Secondary Education Enrolment December-January 1996.

Scholarships, Bursaries and Awards Guide for Aboriginal Students Special Education Training Opportunities

6

Religious education in Pakistan: salvation or subjugation?

FARID PANJWANI

Farid Panjwani analyses the relative power of various stakeholders in shaping the curriculum of Religious Education in Pakistan, the discourses of Islam currently resonating in the education system and the sites of contest and resistance, particularly amongst the young. These issues are situated in the historical trajectory of politics in Pakistan. The attempt to offer a unifying curriculum for Religious Education suggests comparisons with Pinson's account of contemporary Citizenship Education in Israel.

The time has come, the Walrus said. Perhaps things will get worse and then better. Perhaps there's a small god up in heaven readying herself for us. Another world is not only possible, she's on her way. Maybe many of us won't be here to greet her, but on a quiet day, if I listen very carefully, I can hear her breathing. (Arundhati Roy, 2003, p75)

Pakistan is an example of a modern state created in the name of religion. Many of its founders saw religion to be a source of core identity for its people, strong enough to unite diverse cultural traditions and races. Despite the counter evidence of the events in the subsequent history of Pakistan, the perception of religious identity as the source, or at least the intended source, of core identity continues to linger in the type of religious education (RE) provided to students in Pakistan. This paper is concerned with the scope of this religious education and the religiosity[1] nurtured through it, arguing that religious education provides benefits to certain groups that dominate Pakistan's economic and military leadership. The paper also examines a counter-hegemonic discourse within the context of RE by exploring discussions in an e-mail group set up by a group of young men and women. The paper draws upon two fieldwork projects carried out in Karachi, the southern port city.[2] Despite there being a family resemblance among the types of RE provided across Pakistan, there is no claim to generalisation as RE is intimately linked with people's cultures, which vary throughout Pakistan.

Avenues of formal Religious Education

The cultures that make up Pakistan are, by and large, religious. Though a child growing up in such cultures is constantly acquiring religious education, there are at least two formal avenues for instruction in RE in Pakistan: the *madrasas* and the school system. This paper is essentially concerned with RE in the school system, rather than in the *madrasas* – though a brief account of the *madrasas* is provided.

The *madrasas* are the traditional institutions for religious education in a Muslim context, tracing their roots back to the tenth century C.E. (Makdisi, 1981). There are more than 10,000 *madrasas* all over Pakistan offering free education to over a million children.

Since the early eighties, the *madrasas* entered a growth phase, as a result of the combined effect of General Zia's so-called Islamisation and the West's, particularly the United States', backing of his régime. This backing was rooted in Washington's need of Pakistan as an ally in its war against the Soviets in Afghanistan. Since then there has been a phenomenal growth in the number of *madrasas*: from 868 in 1975 to 8000 in 1995 and to more than 10,000 by a recent estimate (Anon., 2001). While state patronage was perhaps the single most significant factor in the growth of *madrasas*, this growth was also a response to the continued failure of the educational system in Pakistan to respond to the needs of the poorest segments of the population.

Though the school system in Pakistan is divided into primary, secondary and tertiary levels, the sociological division between the public and private schools reflects, as well as reinforces, social stratifications. The pervasive influence of religious education can be gaged by the fact that despite huge differences in the public and private systems of education, RE is a compulsory subject in both the systems. (In fact, it is compulsory until the undergraduate level.) To understand the importance of religious education, a glance at the history of the creation of Pakistan is necessary.

Religion and politics in the history of Pakistan

Pakistan came into being on August 14, 1947, comprising two separate geographical areas: East Pakistan, now Bangladesh, and West Pakistan. Separated by about thousand miles, the two areas were on the east and west of India.

Mr. Mohammad Ali Jinnah, the founder of the new nation, put the case for Pakistan in five words, 'The Muslims are a nation.' (Nicholas, 1944, p189). Although Jinnah considered the Muslims to be a separate nation *vis-à-vis* the Hindus, he never believed in an Islamic state or in religion being the driving force for Pakistan. In an interview given to the Reuters's correspondent in New Delhi in 1946 he said,

> The new state would be a modern democratic state with sovereignty resting in the people and the members of the new nation having equal rights of citizenship regardless of their religion, caste or creed. (Munir, 1980, p29)

However, against Jinnah's wishes, there were deeper currents at work that ultimately led to a bringing together of religion and politics in the history of Pakistan.

Between 1757 and 1857 there was a complete reversal of fortunes for the Muslims of South Asia as they lost political power to the British. The period also brought them in touch with an entirely new form of culture, education system, ways of governance, social mores and technological advances. These transformations were coupled by the growing power of the majority Hindu population, over which the Muslims had been ruling for centuries.

From the middle of the nineteenth century to the third decade of the twentieth century, there was a gradual emergence of a Muslim political consciousness (Lapidus, 1988: pp718-748). Up until then parochial family, lineage, caste, regional and class interests and identities commonly overrode Muslimness, though there always was a universalising dimension to Muslim identity, based on the traditional notion of *Ummah* (variously translated as community, nation, and brother-hood). Thus, a new political construct, the Muslims of India, was born (*ibid*).

As the twentieth century progressed, several events reinforced political consciousness among the Muslims. They sought a political platform of their own and got one in 1906 with the founding of the Muslim League. Passing through various phases of co-operation and dissociation with the Hindus, including the Kanpor riots, the *quit India* movement and the *Khilafat* movement, by the late 1930s there was a clear demand by the Muslims for territorial separatism (Ahmad, 1999; Hardy, 1972).

The Muslim League, which by now had emerged as the chief representative of the Muslims, mobilised mass support for the demand for a separate country (Smith, 1946). However, consisting mainly of the landed class, the League did not have roots in the masses. For this, it had to rely on traditional Muslim religious leaders and young students who played a key role in convincing people that their religion would be endangered in a united India after the British withdrawal (Hardy, 1972), thus drawing them to support the demand for a separate country in the name of Islam.

The campaign was successful and the League succeeded in capturing the symbolic attachment to Islam for the purpose of a national political movement, resulting in its winning all the seats reserved for Muslims in the elections of 1946 (Schimmel, 1980). However, as this success came at a price of joining hands with religious groups, it injected the mixture of religion and politics into the veins of the country even before it was born.

The first constitutional impact of religious groups in Pakistan was in the form of the 'Objectives Resolution,' which stated that sovereignty lies with God and not with the people, the opposite of Jinnah's word quoted above. Passed in 1949, just six months after the death of Jinnah, the resolution formed the preamble to all the subsequent constitutions of Pakistan (Ahmed, 1987). From then on the influence of religion in public discourse continued to rise (see Munir, 1980 for a discussion of the historical trajectory). One particular issue that potently reflects this trajectory is the issue of the *Qadianis*. Since the 1950s, most religious groups in Pakistan had been advocating that the

Qadianis should be declared non-Muslims. This is because these religious groups have considered *Qadiani* views about the finality of Prophet Muhammad incongruent with conventional Muslim beliefs. They succeeded in their efforts in 1974, under the ostensibly secular government of Zulfiqar Ali Bhutto.

However, the biggest boon to the religious parties came in the eighties under the rule of General Zia ul-Haq, when Pakistan experienced its longest period of martial law lasting eleven years from 1977 to 1988. During this period, Zia used Islam as political capital and most religious parties joined him in his Islamisation efforts (Faruki, 1987: pp53-78). The current President, General Musharaf, despite initial promises to end religious extremism and promote moderate Islam, has been finding it difficult to curtail the power of the religious parties. In the 2002 elections, riding on the rising wave of anti-American feelings, for the first time in the country's history an alliance of six major religious parties, the *Muttahida Majlie-e-Amal* (MMA), won power in two provinces and in the national assembly (ICG, 2003). Unlike General Zia, Musharaf faces contradictory forces as in the post 9/11 world, the pressure from the United States is to restrain religious extremism rather than to support it, as was the case during Zia's era in the 1980s.

It is important to note that the power of religious groups is also supported by the feudal leaders who continue to dominate Pakistan's political and economic life. More will be said about their role below. (For details of feudalism in Pakistan see Fatima (2000) and Akhtar (2000)).

And yet, despite this escalating role of religion in Pakistan's public life, in reality it never was able to bind the people together: linguistic, racial and ethnic identities constantly challenged and defined people's identity more than religion did. The division of Pakistan into Bangladesh and what now remains as Pakistan, the relentless ethnic tensions and political struggles based on tribes and race are proofs of the failure of religion to provide ideological unity.

Perspectives in Religious Education

Here my concern is to explore the impact of the climate of tension, struggle and ideological disunity upon the mind sets, attitudes, religiosity and perspectives being fostered through religious education and their intellectual and social implications. I will discuss the curricular content to illustrate the deeper issues.

Some of the goals of RE are articulated in official documents (GOP, 2002)[3]. They are to:

- instil certainty about the basic beliefs of Islam in the hearts and minds of students

- foster in students love, greatness and obedience for Allah

- cultivate love for Prophet Muhammad and instil the belief in his finality

- infuse a firm belief in the perfection of Islam in students' hearts and minds

- create a desire to learn the Quran and *Hadith* and follow them

- inform the students about the glorious past of the Muslims

- inform the students about the ideology of Pakistan and create in them love for it

- develop them spiritually and morally in light of Islamic ideals

Embedded in these aims are assumptions about knowledge, religious education, teaching learning and learners. Some 65 years ago Dewey exposed these assumptions:

> The subject-matter of education consists of bodies of information and of skills that have been worked out in the past; therefore, the chief business of the school is to transmit them to the new generation. In the past, there have also been developed standards and rules of conducts in forming habits of actions in conformity with these rules and standards (1938, p17).

The goals also show a theological, moral and doctrinal understanding of Islam restricted to the meaning of *Tawheed* (Oneness of God), finality of the Prophet, Islamic ideals, prayers and service. This is a very narrow understanding of religion. There are cultural, social and humanistic dimensions to religions which are missing here. Consequently, the *Islamiyyat* curriculum does not deal with the literary, artistic and other cultural dimensions of Muslim societies.

Political underpinnings are also visible in the list of goals. For example, the emphasis on the finality of Prophethood resonates with the issue of the *Qadianis*. Recourse to religious teachings for nationalism is another goal whereby regional and ethnic identities are subordinated to that of religion. As we have seen, this is rooted in the very rationale for the creation of Pakistan as a separate nation.

There is a structural similarity of content across the grades. Essentially, the curriculum at any level has the following components, with varying details and subject matter within each component.

* The Quran: This includes memorisation of selected verses with translation and, where necessary, some explanation.

* The *Hadith* and *Sira* (sayings and the life of the Prophet): Students are required to memorise a list of selected sayings of the Prophet and learn about aspects of his life. The selection usually reflects the goals of the curriculum.

* Ethics and Worship: This section consists of short essays on selected themes such as service, patience, honesty, prayers, fasting, and pilgrimage.

* History: This section includes essays on aspects of Islamic Law, achievements of Muslims and short biographies of pre-Islamic prophets and close associates of Prophet Muhammad.

Presentation of history

Writing the history of a religion, particularly by the religious community itself, is a challenging task. It needs to avoid the extremes of mythologisation as well as a reductionist presentation of the past. In doing so, it has to explore the relationship of the function of the sacred to historical interests and struggles. This curriculum does not do this.

The presentation of *Sharia* – the standard term used for Muslim law – in the curriculum is a good example to consider. It is presented as a divine law applicable to all times and given as a complete set of instructions. There is no discussion of its historical emergence and its gradual expansion throughout its history to incorporate more and more facets of social activity that were clearly not foreseeable in the Quran. In the same vein, the curriculum presents the theological developments in Islam – for example of the notion of *Tawheed* – as uniform doctrines that have been preserved right from the time of the Prophet. The historicity of doctrines and the variety of interpretations and internal differences in Muslim history are simply ignored. The thought, practice and impact of the *Sufis* as well as other minorities such as the *Shias* are not portrayed at all, except in the form of some anecdotes of piety, and humility.

There is a consideration of the differences between the *Shia* and the *Sunni* historical trajectories. However, it is portrayed in a manner likely to be damaging to the religious perspectives of students: instead of presenting these differences positively recognising the diversity within Islam, it emphasises rifts and differences. The *Sunni* view is presented as normative and the *Shia* perspective comes across as a 'branching off' from the mainstream.

Until grade VIII, there is a uniform curriculum for all the students. In grade IX, the common curriculum is divided into two separate curricula for the *Shia* and *Sunni* students. According to a curriculum writer, this happened after the *Shia* religious scholars repeatedly protested against the lack of the *Shia* point of view in the curriculum on Muslim history after the death of the Prophet. Correspondingly, in grade IX, students have to make a choice between studying the *Shia* or the *Sunni* sections. It is this divisive manner of the study of Muslim history, and the implicit association of *Sunni* with normative and mainstream Islam, that can lead to segregation rather than integration. It seems that the arrangement seeks to 'protect' the mainstream *Sunni* students from the 'contamination' of *Shia* doctrines!

Thus the curriculum presents the norms and phenomena of Muslim societies *a*historically, which can lead to their reification. Such reification is among the hallmarks of absolutism. Without historical appreciation of the movement of thought, norms and practices, it is easy for students to fall for absolutist theories and extremist religio-political ideologies, as they will not have the intellectual tools to assess their claims.

Monolithic hermeneutics

The entire school system in Karachi revolves around the centrality of textbooks. While this is true for almost all the subjects, it is particularly visible in RE classes. This may be due to at least two addi-

92

tional factors. First, the teachers of RE are among the least qualified teachers. The second factor pertains to the political sensitivities associated with the subject matter. Both of these factors can force a teacher to play 'safe' and thus remain close to the text. For example, while the textbook is full of quotations in Arabic, most teachers have no knowledge of Arabic. Thus the translations and interpretations of the Quran and the *Hadith* given in the textbook are accepted as the right and only possible versions of these texts. A good example of this is the discussion of the 'Day of Judgement' found in the textbook of grade VIII (pp10-13). The discussion in the book is a straightforward advocacy of a particular interpretation of the concept: physical resurrection, accountability of deeds done in this life and punishment. Now, in the history of the Muslims, the verses of the Quran referring to the 'Day of Judgement' have been interpreted in many ways and there was a vigorous debate around the viability of the notion of physical resurrection. All these twists and turns and lived realities of history are steamrollered in the book.

As textbooks contain extracts from the most sacred texts for the Muslims, the Quran and the *Hadith*, this reverence of text in religious education creates a double demand for textual reverence obliterating possibilities of critical engagement both on the part of teachers and the students. The force of this influence is augmented by the impact of the examination system. It is widely believed that the more literally a student quotes from the textbook, the higher will be the grades. This centrality of the text may lead to a disproportional importance being given to them as a source of religious knowledge and guidance. Text can replace conscience: it can absolve the reader, and in this case the follower of a religion, from taking personal responsibility for moral and political decisions. Such reliance on the role of the author as the producer of meanings is yet another characteristic of absolutist ideologies and the way texts are utilised in religious education in Karachi sub-consciously prepares students to fall prey to them.

Religious education and religiosity

William James, in his classic *Varieties of Religious Experiences* (1902), distinguishes between religious geniuses and people with second-hand religions. The former are the founders of great religions, the saints and others who appear to have a direct consciousness of the divine. The second-hand religious people are those who follow the conventional observances; their religion has been made for them by others, communicated to them by tradition, determined for them by imitation and retained by habit. According to James, these are the majority in any religious tradition.

Examining the issue of religiosity some hundred years later, Abdul Karim Soroush, a well-known Iranian scholar, distinguishes among imitative, gnostic and mystic types of religiosities (Soroush, 2000). His mystic type is similar to James's religious geniuses and his imitative religiosity comes close to James's second-hand religiosity. He characterises the latter as habitual, ritualistic, fatalistic, collective and obedient. The gnostic type is in between the two, but not necessarily more balanced and superior; it has neither the ritualistic attachment of the imitators nor the direct consciousness of the mystics. It rather spends time in intellectualising religion, engaging in drawing pleasure out of doctrinal quibbling, textual interpretations and the nit pickings of theologies. Like James, Soroush privileges the mystic over other types of religiosities.

If we apply this analysis to religious education in Karachi, it is clear that it produces religiosity that is the second-hand and imitative type. Students nurtured in such a religiosity can be easily manipulated provided they are persuaded that what they have been asked to do is in the name of religion.

Who benefits?

The above type of RE and its underlying religiosity is perpetuated, as it benefits certain groups. The first set of groups is internal to Pakistani society and the last group is external.

The traditional religious clerics

In most newspapers in Pakistan there is a regular page devoted to traditional religious scholars responding to the questions asked by readers. The *madrasa* of Binoria in Karachi has a webpage devoted to people seeking advice on day-to-day matters (Binoria, undated). These print and electronic pages are perfect indicators of the imitative and ritualistic type of religiosity discussed above.

If Islam is a comprehensive blueprint, providing direction in all aspects of human life, one needs only to ask those who posses the blueprint for a recipe for any situation in life. For these 'knowledgeable' people religion becomes identity and they defend it as they would defend their homeland, property or life. A monolithic approach to the meaning of text, together with the lack of historical context and the centrality of the text itself, all combine to ensure that the traditional religious cleric-class benefit from the perpetuation of imitative and ritualistic religiosity.

Feudal lords

The role of feudalism in Pakistan's politics was mentioned above. The class consists of landlords with large joint families in possession of thousands of acres of land. The work on their lands is done by peasants or tenants who live at subsistence level. Such a system can not derive legitimacy from any institution that fosters freedom of thought and intellect, and freedom of speech and expression.

The system derives its legitimacy through its endorsement by a religious clergy which sustains an imitative and ritualistic religiosity. The feudal system interprets all the commands to acquire knowledge in the foundational texts of Islam as referring to knowledge about religion only. It is in their interest that their peasants acquire education, by which they mean religious education, which emphasises obedience and fatalism, and which truly serves as 'opium for the masses'.

Military

The third group that benefits from the above mentioned type of religiosity is the military. They have benefited because nationalism in Pakistan has always sought to define itself against the Indian/Hindu other (Jaffrelot, 2002). The fact that India has a Hindu majority and that Pakistan emphasises Islam as a source of its national identity, provides the necessary means by which national antagonisms are confluent with religious distinctions. The military class of Pakistan continuously justifies its existence and the immense resources it consumes by appealing to this collective and ahistorical confluence of religion and nationality.

The western hegemony

The fourth group that benefits from this religiosity is the establishments and hegemonic powers in the West, particularly the United States. There is a clear relationship between efforts to create a docile population, supporting dictatorships and the interests of global capitalist powers and collaborating states (Roy, 2003; Chomsky, 1983). In the case of Pakistan, the example of the patronage received by General Zia ul-Haq and his policies of Islamisation are sufficient indicators of this link. However, the tragic events of September 11 have put these hegemonic powers in a quandary. They now want Pakistan and other countries to curb and control the growth of absolutist ideologies, yet they would not want a critical education system to replace it which could lead to a politically conscious and active citizenry. How this dilemma plays itself out in the context of religious education needs to be considered.[4]

Where is the resistance?

It might appear that the perpetuation of powerful groups helped by the religious education in Pakistan means the chances of any meaningful resistance are poor. There is no doubt that the increasingly hegemonic stance of the US in the post-9/11 world has strengthened the internal groups mentioned above. The fourth group, however, now sees the growing powers of religious parties as a threat. By now the roots of religious fundamentalism have grown deep and attempts by the West to curb them through force are likely to lead to a stronger opposition.

Sites of resistance exist which point to the smouldering desire for freedom, for rationality, for peace, for truth lying in the deepest recesses of human nature. One such site is the mind and spirit of the youth. During recent classroom observations we saw this spirit at work. The curriculum does not attempt to explore social or intellectual issues faced by Muslims today. Nevertheless, some issues did come up in the class, brought about by the penetrating questions posed by the students. However, a sterile curriculum and dogmatic instructional strategy gradually quelled this passion, at least for the majority. Today, however, this passion has found another path for its fulfilment: the growing interconnectedness of the world through information technology.

In 2002, a group of boys and girls who came together in a non-formal educational institution, created an e-mail group. The group consisted mostly of high school and university students. There were thirty five students in the group, about half of whom participated actively in the e-discussions. The students were mostly from urban, middle and lower middle income groups.

The group discussed various issues of interest and over time started to engage in exploring religious and social issues as well. A friend of mine who was part of the group, through his association with the non-formal educational institution, invited me to participate in these social and religious discussions.

I will focus on the group's discussion of religious pluralism to indicate how it allowed the members to think through issues and raise matters unthinkable to the perpetuators of the religious education discussed above.

Religious pluralism is a thorny issue, raising fundamental questions about the truth claims of religions. It is dealt with obliquely in the curriculum under consideration. In this curriculum Islam is presented as the last, final and only pure message of Allah. *Allah had sent prophets and books to communities in the past as well. However, the teachings of these prophets and the books revealed to them are no longer in their original condition.* (Textbook for class IX and X). Thus, Islam is portrayed as a perfect and complete message of the series of messages sent by Allah for the guidance of humankind. The curriculum acknowledges the truth claim of revelations prior to it but sees them abrogated after the revelation of Islam. There is a discussion of preaching and conversion in the curriculum but it does not take into account the issues of religious plurality surrounding us today (Textbook of class VIII, pp 47ff).

How did the e-mail group explore this issue? The discussion began when one member suggested that in view of the predominance gained by the term pluralism in the current discourses, we should explore it and its consequences for religion. After some initial comments, I tried to explain the conditions that have contributed to making pluralism an important idea.

> Perhaps one way to approach the issue is to try and trace the origins of the predominance of the idea of pluralism... Pluralism becomes

an important idea in a world where there is a kind of over-exposure to the other, and this other cannot be obliterated/ vanquished/ assimilated. It becomes a non-dissolvable reality. That is when pluralism becomes important.

Next was an e-mail that argued that if we accept pluralism then all religions, including Islam, are guilty of being unpluralistic through their attempts to convert.

If we agree that there r 2 ways of reaching a point and both r unique and each has its own pros and cons then y do I need to convince the person following the other path to follow mine?

This was taken forward by another member who wrote:

Now leave our religious biases aside and think over it in a little depth: What the Muslim fundamentalist are doing today, is it pluralist in nature? Just think in detail. I m not against *dawah* (preaching); in particular what I want to say is that by taking the position on pluralism today we are somehow implying *dawah* and hence conversion efforts to be baseless.

At this stage one member tried to distinguish between past and present. She argued that we may be anachronistic in applying the theory of pluralism to a time when the geo-political situation was very different and such concepts were not prevalent nor were conditions such as they are today. By historicising the issue she was trying to salvage the conversion attempts of the past. This, however, raised issues of relativity of values, another topic discussed by the group.

Yet another response to the above quote was that although conversion itself was not anti-pluralistic, forced conversion was. The argument was that people who believed in pluralism as a value also tried to convert others to their viewpoint. In response to this one participant wrote:

But does pluralism means only change in behaviour or a change in conviction as well? I mean, is it ok to carry on being convinced of your superior belief while pretending and behaving that others also have equally legitimate believes?

This thought has the potential to lead to an almost opposite conclusion about religious belief than what is advocated in the textbooks. This led to the exploration of pluralism and relativism and the limits of pluralism. The discussions on pluralism continued for more than a month during which about ninety e-mails were exchanged within the group.

In these harbingers of change I hear the breathing of Arundhati Roy's small god.

Notes

1   Religiosity is understood as the attitude towards religion, religious beliefs and tradition. Current research in the psychology of religion has argued for different types of religiosities (Hackney and Sanders, 2003)
2   The paper is partly based on fieldworks conducted in 1996 and 2001; see Karim and Panjwani (1996)
3   Religious Education is called *Islamiyyat* in Karachi. Henceforth the two terms will be used interchangeably.
4   A recent example of such pressure is the outcome of the 2003 annual meeting of the Gulf Cooperation Council that agreed on new measures to combat terrorism, including purging rhetoric from school textbooks that Washington says fuels anti-western sentiments (Haddadin, 2003).

Bibliography

Ahmad, A (1999) *Studies in Islamic Culture in the Indian Environment.* Delhi: Oxford University Press
Ahmed, I (1987) *The concept of an Islamic State: an analysis of the ideological controversy in Pakistan.* Lahore: Pinter Press
Akhtar, S (2000) *Media, Religion and Politics in Pakistan.* Oxford: OUP
Anon, (2001) [Online] Available from http://www.rediff.com/news/2001/aug/21pak1.htm. [Accessed: 18 January 2004]
Binoria (undated) [Online] Available from http://www.binoria.org/qanda/listing.html [Accessed: 18 January 2004]
Chomsky, N (1983) *The Culture of Terrorism.* Boston: South End Press
Dewey, J (1938) *Experience and Education.* London: Macmillan
Faruki, K (1987) Pakistan: Islamic Government and Society, in: Eposito (ed.) *Islam in Asia: Religion, Politics and Society.* Oxford and New York: Oxford University Press
Fatima, M (2000) Feudalism: a myth or mother of all ills?, in: *Daily Dawn,* January 31 [Online] Available from http://www.dawn.com/2000/01/31/ebr12.htm [Accessed: 18 January 2004]
Haddadin, H (2003) *Financial Times* [Online] Available from: http://news.ft.com/servlet/ContentServer?pagename=FT.com/WireFeed/WireFeedandc=WireFeedandcid=1069495593590andp=1014232938216. [Accessed: 18 January 2004]
Government of Pakistan (2002) *Nisab-e-Islamiyat (lazmi) jamat nahum wa dahum* (trans. Syllabus of Islamiyat (compulsory) for classes IX and X). Curriculum Wing, Ministry of Education

Hackney, C and Sanders, G (2003) Religiosity and Mental Health: A Meta-Analysis of Recent Findings, in: *Journal for the Scientific Study of Religion*, 42(1): 43-55

Hardy, P (1972) *The Muslims of British India*. London: Cambridge University Press

International Crisis Group (2003) *Pakistan: The Mullahs and the Military*. Islamabad: Brussels

Jaffrelot, C (2002) *Nationalism without a Nation*. New Delhi, Manohar

James, W (1902) *Varieties of Religious Experiences*. New York: Longman, Green

Karim, F and Panjwani, F (1996) Religious Education: Curriculum, pedagogy and teaching-learning environment in the Secondary schools of Dhaka and Karachi with special reference to the teaching of Islam. (Unpublished)

Lapidus, I (1988) *A History of Islamic Societies*. Cambridge: Cambridge University Press

Makdisi, G (1981) *The rise of colleges: institutions of learning in Islam and the West*. Edinburgh: Edinburgh University Press

Munir, M (1980) *From Jinnah to Zia*. Lahore: Vanguard Books

Nicholas, B (1944) *Verdict on India*. London: Jonathan Cape

Roy, Arundhati (2003) *War Talk*. Cambridge, MA: South End Press

Schimmel, A (1980) *Islam in the Indian Subcontinent*. Leiden: Brill

Smith, W (1946) *Islam in Modern India*. London: Gollancz

Sindh Textbook Board (undated) *Islamiyat Syllabus for Secondary Classes*

Sindh Textbook Board *Islamiyyat Textbooks for classes VI-X*

Soroush, A (2000) Types of Religiosity, in Kiyan, issue 50. [Online] Available from:http://www.drsoroush.com/English/Articles/2000_Types_of_Religiousity.htm [Accessed: 18 January 2004]

7

Citizenship education in Israel: between democracy and Jewishness – dilemmas of policy-makers

HALLELI PINSON

Following Panjwani's deconstruction of the Islamic Studies curriculum in Pakistan, Halleli Pinson turns to the discourses which have shaped Citizenship Education in Israel. Through an analysis of interviews with Ministry of Education officials, Pinson explores the conflicting notions of Israeli citizenship which underpin the new curriculum, and the discourses of nationhood and identity which make the creation of an inclusive curriculum across all sectors of Israeli education highly problematic. The oppositions and tensions described here, and the privileging of dominant identities within a supposedly inclusive system, foreshadow McNiff's arguments in favour of an agonistic basis for peace education in the final chapter in this section.

Introduction

During the last few decades we have witnessed a growing interest in Citizenship Education in terms of both policy and research. In recent years new approaches to Citizenship Education have emerged. If until recently the dominant approaches to Citizenship Education were 'thin' or minimal (McLaughlin, 1992), mainly emphasising the need to provide the students with knowledge about the political system, today there has been a shift towards broader, maximal, approaches which highlight aspects such as participation, identity and membership in a community (Evans, 1998; Kennedy, 1997; McLaughlin, 1992). Moreover it is now possible to identify a new consensus among scholars, educationalists and politicians regarding the need for Citizenship Education (Beck, 1998; Carr, 1991; Davies *et al*, 1999; Evans, 1998; Pearce and Hallgarten, 2000). Indeed Citizenship Education has become a much-emphasised area in the school curriculum in many countries (Derricott, 1998). Israel in this sense is no exception. In recent years Citizenship Education in Israel has been undergoing some major changes, with the prospect of creating a more inclusive Citizenship Education curriculum that would stress ideas such as pluralistic and democratic citizenship. In 1994 new curriculum guidelines for Citizenship Education were published (Ministry of Education, 1994) followed six years later by the official textbook, *To be citizens in Israel: A Jewish and democratic state* (Ministry of Education, 2000a). The new citizenship curriculum was implemented first in September 2000 in Jewish schools (Ministry of Education, 2000b) then in September 2001 in Arab schools (Ministry of Education, 2001).

This chapter seeks to explore potential tensions that might emerge from the process of designing and executing an inclusive Citizenship Education curriculum in Israel. The data presented here draw on thirteen in-depth interviews conducted between April and August 2001 with officials at the Ministry of Education who were involved in Citizenship Education. Of the 13 officials interviewed, three were Arabs/Palestinians, four were religious Jews who work in the religious state education sector, and the rest were secular Jews. Three of the officials were supervisors for Citizenship Education in the three state educational sectors: general, Arab and religious. Two were involved in the process of shaping the curriculum and the curriculum material and eight were teachers' advisors who were responsible for the implementation of the new curriculum. Two of the eight advisors were also involved in writing the official textbook.

The analysis in this chapter focuses in particular on a) the ways in which the officials discursively constituted the notion of Israeli citizenship that Citizenship Education in Israel should promote, and b) how the task of creating an inclusive Citizenship Education in a nationally and religiously segregated society and educational system was tackled. I begin by outlining the socio-political context of Citizenship Education in Israel. I then analyse the notion of Israeli citizenship that underpins the official discourses of Citizenship Education. In the second half of this chapter I discuss how the tensions between inclusion and exclusion are perceived by the officials I interviewed.

The myth of Israeli citizenship and the Citizenship curriculum

Three prominent factors can be identified as shaping the nature of Israeli citizenship: security concerns; the conflict between the state of Israel and the Palestinians and between Israel and its neighbouring Arab states; the social divisions in Israeli society along the lines of nationality, ethnicity, religion and class; and finally, the inherent tension between Israel's character as a democratic state and its particularistic definition as Jewish nation-state. As a democratic state, Israel is committed to provide equal individual rights to all its citizens, regardless of their origin or religion, while at the same time it has acted to maintain its nature as a Jewish state and to preserve its Jewish majority. The imaginary boundaries of the Israeli collective are constructed first and foremost in terms of belonging to the Jewish people, rather than according to universal civil criteria. Kimmerling (2001) argues that while the Palestinian minority in Israel might be granted access to the material resources of the society as individuals, since the identity of the state has been constructed as Jewish, Palestinian citizens are constantly excluded from the symbolic resources of Israeli society and from participating in discussions about its common good.

Shafir and Peled (2002) suggest that the political culture in Israel, in relation to citizenship, is made up of a struggle between three different, and sometimes interrelated, political discourses: liberal-democratic, republican, and ethno-national, which they define as:

> interested not in civil society, but in a different kind of community: the nation or ethnic group. In the ethno-nationalist, or volkisch, approach, citizenship is not an expression of individual rights or of contribution to the common good, but of membership in a homogenous descent group. The community, in this view, is not conceived of as existing outside the state, or over against it in some way, but rather as expressed in and embodied by the state. (2002:6)

They argue that this creates several mechanisms which generate a hierarchical structure of membership in the polity. The liberal-democratic discourse is used to distinguish between citizens and those who are not citizens, such as the Palestinians in the occupied territories. The republican-Zionist discourse, which was the dominant discourse in Israeli society until the late 1970s, is used to determine the hierarchical position of different Jewish groups, based on their alleged contribution to the Zionist project. Finally, the ethno-national discourse is employed to create a distinction between Jewish citizens who belong to the Israeli citizenship as a collective, and Palestinian citizens who are being included merely as individuals, based on the liberal discourse, but excluded as a group.

The tension between democracy and Jewish particularism has left its mark on the Israeli education system, as well as on the Citizenship Education it offers. The State Education Act of 1953, which is perhaps the most important landmark in the formation of the Israeli educational system, stressed values such as freedom and equality, alongside the commitment to uphold the Jewishness of the state and to use education as a vehicle for strengthening Jewish collective memory and myths. Lemish (2003) suggests that the Act is an example of what Laclau and Mouffe (2001) call hegemonic formation.

The Israeli education system is divided into four main sectors, each serving a different group in Israeli society: the general state school sector, which serves the secular Jewish majority; the Arab state school sector; the Zionist-religious state school sector; and the independent ultra-religious Jewish sector. This sector is recognised by, but not part of, the state school sector, and hence its schools are not fully supported or controlled by the Ministry of Education. These four sectors differ in their levels of autonomy and the state resources they enjoy, depending upon the extent to which the social groups they serve are perceived as located at the centre or the margins of the Israeli collective. The Arab sector, for example, not only suffers from lack of state resources, but also does not enjoy the same autonomy, especially with regard to its curricula, that other separate educational systems, such as the religious Jewish schools, enjoy (Abu-Asba, 1997; Al-Haj, 1994). Therefore, to a significant extent, the nationally and religiously segregated education system in Israel reproduces the position of groups in Israeli society.

In the light of these facts, one should ask what sort of Citizenship Education can this education system offer, and what might be its aims? Until the late 1970s Citizenship Education was part of the

Jewish history curriculum in all state secondary schools. Indeed, its aim at that time was first and foremost to promote the Zionist agenda. In 1976 Citizenship Education was introduced for the first time as a separate compulsory curriculum subject for both secular and religious Jewish state high schools, and in 1979 this curriculum was 'adapted' to 'fit' the Arab sector. However, in practice, in each of the state education sectors a different curriculum was implemented, using different textbooks. By and large, the 1976 curriculum, and the textbooks that were written for its implementation in Israeli schools, put the Jewish-Zionist ethos at the centre of Citizenship Education (Pinson, 2000).

A decade after the implementation of the first compulsory Citizenship curriculum in Israel, the need to re-think Citizenship Education was raised. As Popkewitz and Brennan point out, moves of this sort are always part of a wider pattern:

> Reforms in education do not occur in a vacuum, but are intricately connected to activity in other fields (1999:22).

During the 1980s changes in Israeli society, such as the new popularity gained by *Kach*, a Jewish racist political party, and increasing expressions of political intolerance between Palestinian and Jewish citizens and between left and right wings, brought issues such as democratic education to the fore of the educational agenda. In 1989 the Minister for Education put together a new curriculum committee for Citizenship Education with the prospect of designing a new, more inclusive and more democratically oriented Citizenship curriculum

The main innovations of the committee, which completed its work in 1994, were the recommendation to create, for the first time, one unified curriculum for all state high schools (i.e. general, religious Jewish and Arab schools) and to construct Citizenship Education as a vehicle for social change. The committee explicitly called for the education system to endorse a more inclusive notion of Citizenship Education. In a radical departure from the former influences of the hierarchical structure of Israeli citizenship, the Curriculum Committee concluded:

> The new curriculum offers a broad common citizenship notion to all students... Thus there is no justification for maintaining separate curricula for the different state school sectors (Ministry of Education, 1994:4-5, author's translation).

However, this progressive language with its implications of inclusivity contrasts with the following aim in the 1994 curriculum guidelines:

> Students should also acknowledge the existence of the Israeli state as the state of the Jewish people and understand its commitment to the Jewish people in the diasporas (*ibid*: 7, author's translation).

To a great extent, the 1994 Citizenship curriculum and its accompanying textbook *To Be Citizens in Israel: A Jewish and Democratic State* (Ministry of Education, 2000a), which I shall call from now on *To Be Citizens*, shifted from a monolithic Jewish-Zionist interpretation of Israeli citizenship to a more pluralistic approach (Pinson, 2000). Yet the current curriculum does not operate in a vacuum, and the tensions emerging from the characteristics of Israel as both Jewish and democratic are ever present. In the remainder of this chapter I will examine how officials in the Ministry of Education perceived these tensions, and what discourses they deployed in addressing them. (Extracts from interviews presented here are translated by the author; the interviews were conducted in Hebrew.)

Citizenship Education in a Jewish and democratic state

Israeli scholars suggest that, if until the late 1970s the dominant discourse in Israel was the republican, today the main struggle in Israeli political culture is between individualistic liberal-democratic interpretations and ethno-national discourses of citizenship (Kimmerling, 2001; Shafir and Peled, 2002). Resnik's (1999) study on Israeli school curricula identified four national images that were deployed in different historical periods: a) a nation with a right to a state b) a nation with a right to religion c) a state for a persecuted people d) and a state for all its citizens. These different images, Resnik claims, represent the tensions between universalistic liberal ideas and Jewish particularism.

My own analysis of the 1994 curriculum and *To Be Citizens* (Pinson, 2000) suggests that this curriculum is caught between the aspiration to create an inclusive Citizenship Education that would draw upon democratic-liberal discourse, and the wish for the state of Israel and its educational system to maintain its Jewish nature and its commitment to the Jewish people. This resulted in both the 1994 curriculum guidelines and *To Be Citizens* adopting an ambivalent or hybrid approach (Dussel *et al*, 2000; Popkewitz, 2000) as to the type of Citizenship Education Israel should endorse. A salient example can be

found in the way *To Be Citizens* discusses the different approaches to
the definition of the state of Israel:

> The different approaches in relation to the definition of the State of
> Israel could be presented on a continuum. At one end one can find
> the approach of the state of Israel as a Torah State ... At the other
> end one can find the approach of the state of Israel as a state of all
> its citizens ... Between these two ends one can find the Zionist
> approaches which acknowledge the fact that the State of Israel is a
> Jewish and democratic state. (Ministry of Education, 2000a:29-30,
> author's translation).

Despite the fact that *To Be Citizens* offers students the opportunity to
examine different interpretations of the definition of the state of
Israel, the ways in which the discussion is constructed suggests that
the textbook takes a clear stance in relation to the desirable definition
of Israeli citizenship. By introducing an imaginary continuum, the
textbook also draws clear borders between the Zionist interpretations
which are located at the centre, and approaches which reject either the
character of the state as Jewish or as democratic, and thus are pushed
to the margins.

When the officials I interviewed discussed the aims of Citizenship
Education, it seemed they all agreed, whatever their religion or
national affiliation, that the definition of the state of Israel which
Citizenship Education should promote is the dual definition of Israel
as an ethnic-nation state and as a democratic state. However, a more
careful reading of their responses reveals a diversity of interpretations
that to some extent reflects the hybridisation of approach to Israeli
citizenship that was found in the official teaching materials.

For some of the officials, the purpose behind Citizenship Education is
to engage the students in discussions concerning the special characteristics and problematics that emerge from the dual definition of the
state of Israel. As Official 2 explained:

> The state of Israel is a Jewish and democratic state, these are the
> principles it was established upon, and this is what it declares ...
> The textbook is based on this approach and the dispute, the
> ambivalence, not the ambivalence but the contradictions between
> Jewish and democratic state that sometimes happen not always, but
> many times. This is also something that is discussed in classrooms
> and it does not mean that we reach a conclusion in classrooms,
> because there is no resolution in Israeli society (Official 2).

For Official 2 the definition of Israel as both Jewish and democratic embodies many problems and contradictions. Seeing this as the framework for Citizenship Education should be interpreted as an opportunity to discuss these tensions. Other officials understood the dual definition of Israeli citizenship in terms of a topic for discussion as well as a set of values that Citizenship Education should promote:

> The message of the curriculum is that we believe that it is possible to be both a Jewish and a democratic state. This means that this is what we educate towards. However, we still bring views of those who think it is not possible, but it goes without saying that the focus of the textbook is this approach (Official 9).

It was very interesting in this context to see the responses of the Arab officials and the ways in which they defined the framework of Citizenship Education.

> When we designed the curriculum one of the things that I had no choice but to accept is the definition of Israel as a nation-state, as the state of the Jewish nation ... It is not only the case of the rule of the majority but this is one of the principles that Israel was established upon ... In one sentence the curriculum emphasises two things related to the character of the state. Its character as a Jewish and democratic state. This is the main emphasis and the rest of the issues the curriculum discusses derive from it ... In the Arab schools the emphasis is more about the democratic aspect and the problems the Arab minority has to face as a national minority that lives in a state with an ethnic and democratic nature (Official 13).

Here Official 13 expresses his support for using the definition of Israel as a Jewish and democratic state as the framework for Citizenship Education. The way the Arab officials reconciled the contradiction they experienced between their beliefs regarding the desirable character of Israel and its current definition was by constructing the need to study the Jewish nature of Israel as a means of understanding the status and the problems of the Palestinian minority. In this respect the responses of Arab officials can be seen as a form of resistance to the hegemonic discourse, and an attempt to use its framework to empower their students.

On the other hand, some of the officials stressed the priority of the Zionist interpretation of Israeli citizenship over alternative approaches:

The aim is to develop critical thinking but also very explicitly to accept and legitimate the state's framework as a Jewish and democratic state ... I mean there is no one who wants to go to a format of anti-state or to give up the framework of a Jewish state for a format of a state of all its citizens ... The aim really is to identify with the state of Israel as a Jewish state (Official 1).

Here Official 1 sees the aims of Citizenship Education as being to encourage critical thinking among the students. Nonetheless, drawing heavily on ethno-national discourse and what Resnik (1999) identifies as particularistic national images, Official 1 constructs the dual definition of the state of Israel as the *only* acceptable approach while excluding any other alternatives, which this official refers to as 'anti-state'. However, combining the intention to develop critical thinking with the reinforcement of the Zionist interpretation of citizenship suggests that Official 1 is ambivalent in relation to the type of Citizenship Education Israel should endorse. In contrast to the majority of officials, this official does not address directly the potential tensions inherent in the Jewishness of the state.

Even though the majority of officials recognised that the dual definition of Israel is not conflict free, they still insisted on, or accepted, as in the case of the Arab officials, this definition as the framework for Citizenship Education. Examining the ways in which they justified this decision can be revealing in terms of the discourses they drew upon. In a typical response Official 12 explains:

The state of Israel was defined as Jewish nation-state. This is *the decision of the UN* ... There are states in which the identity is a political identity, nationality is a political nationality, citizenship and nationality are the same ... On the other hand in nation-states where their identity, where their national identity is ethnic, so there is a separation between nationality, the ethnic-nationality and the citizenship, *like Belgium* ... The same goes for Israel. There is the national identity of the state as a Jewish state, and there is the citizenship identity ... I mean there was in 1947 the UN decision that says that there will be two nation-states here. Not nation in the political sense, but ethnic-nationality. Two ethnic nation-states: A Jewish nation-state and a Palestinian nation-state ... Especially today with the post-Zionists we say to the students remember where we started from, we started from the UN decision, *the state of Israel wasn't born in a sin* (Official 12, author's emphases).

Official 12 acknowledges the potential challenge that the link between the state of Israel and Jewish nationality and between citizenship and nationhood might pose, especially for the democratic character of the state. This official reconciles this potential challenge by looking for external sources of justification – it is the UN decision – and by suggesting that students should be told that there is nothing unique about the relationship between Israeli citizenship and the Jewish people – it is like Belgium. In doing so, Official 12 employs the national image which Resnik (1999) refers to as ' a nation with a right to a state' and therefore universalises the unique relationship between Israeli citizenship and the Jewish people. Billing (1995) points out that the 'universal' assumption that each nation should have its own state is an example of how the particular is being universalised. By and large this method was also employed in *To Be Citizens*. For example, where *To Be Citizens* discusses the 1950 Law of Return, which is one of the most central pieces of legislation in terms of the definition of Israel as a Jewish state, it reads:

> Many people see the Law of Return as the heart of the Zionist ideal and of the Zionist state. In this law, the founders of the state seek to implement the idea of 'the natural right' of each Jew to live in his own state, if he wishes to ... The aim of the Law of Return is to execute the goal that was set by the Declaration of Independence: to establish a state for the Jewish people (Ministry of Education, 2000a:266).

To Be Citizens, in a somewhat paradoxical way, explains the importance of the Law of Return by drawing upon liberal-democratic language, it is an expression of the 'natural right' of each Jew.

However, universalising the link between nationality and citizenship was not the only way officials suggested that students should understand the relationship between Israeli citizenship and the Jewish people, as the following response demonstrates:

> As soon as they get familiar with the Nationality Law they know what it is to be an Israeli citizen. The Judaism gives the essence and the democracy gives the framework. Now there are duties and rights which are neutral, that apply to any human being. Now citizenship essence, I mean the content, this he gets through the character of the state as a Jewish state and through the democracy, but citizenship itself is something technical (Official 5).

Here, drawing upon ethno-national discourse and an image of 'a nation with a right to religion', Official 5 argues that students should understand the Jewishness of the state as the essence of Israeli citizenship, and that membership in the Israeli polity has no meaning without its link to Jewish nationality – otherwise it is merely technical.

The responses above demonstrate that the relationship between nationhood, the Jewishness of the state, and citizenship, whether it was constructed as a universal relationship or a particular phenomenon, was seen by the officials as a salient concept for Citizenship Education. Interestingly, this link between nationality and citizenship was also understood as an important component of Citizenship Education by the Arab officials.

> One of the aims is alongside the civic education, to educate for nationhood. Or at least the curriculum is structured in a way that the aims of citizenship education are also to nurture the individual identity of the student. In the same way that a Jewish citizen cannot be anything but Jewish, the same goes for the Arab citizen who cannot be anything else but Arab. So if I want to follow this principle I must make sure I will also educate for national identity otherwise I dehumanise the student (Official 8).

For the Arab officials, Citizenship Education is not complete without referring to the students' other identities, and first and foremost, their national identity. The importance they attributed to nationhood as part of Citizenship Education can either be seen as an attempt to incorporate students' differences into the concept of Israeli citizenship, or as the need to resist the strong link between belonging to the Jewish collective and Israel citizenship that has been created by the majority. However, one must ask whether this link was sufficiently challenged by the Arab officials.

Towards inclusive Citizenship Education?

Contemporary Citizenship Education in Israel, as it emerged from the 1994 curriculum guidelines, was designed to offer a more inclusive notion of Israeli citizenship within a hierarchical and segregated system. Further, it was intended to counter these forces. However, despite these aims, as demonstrated in the previous section, the links between citizenship, nationhood and the Jewishness of the state, which

111

entail an exclusive concept of membership in the Israeli state, are still dominant ideas in the official discourses of Citizenship Education.

As the Jewish officials negotiated the different meanings of membership in Israeli society, some of them appeared to be torn between the notion of citizenship identity as common to all, and what belonging to the Israeli collective meant to them:

> I think that *citizenship is the common thing to all of us* and we need to educate people to accept the other, and to understand that he is also a citizen. *The other I mean the one that is not part of the Jewish collective*, he is an equal citizen ... Look, what is a Jewish state is something that also the Arab and Druze sectors should understand, to be familiar with the reality because the state is theirs ... But there isn't any aspiration to educate them according to the Jewish values. *They need to be educated according to universal values* ... On the other hand, the Jewish student, it is obvious that the emphasis is different. It is very important that they will be exposed to, and will know what are the disputes in the public sphere (Official 10, author's emphases).

Official 10 argues here that everyone should be educated for common citizenship, but at the same time distinguishes between two different aims of Citizenship Education: one for Jewish students, which is based on developing a sense of belonging to the Jewish collective; and the other for non-Jewish students, that would derive from a liberal-democratic approach. By drawing upon these distinctions, Official 10 effectively defines two types of Citizenship Education, which to a great extent correspond with the hierarchical structure of Israeli citizenship (Shafir and Peled, 2002).

Official 11 also distinguishes between two types of citizens: those who are included, based on their national identity, in the collective 'we', and those who are excluded and only entitled to be included as individuals based on a liberal notion of citizenship.

> We try in our view of citizenship to express the fact that we are one people and that there is here also another people, we are committed to equality, but we also have to be committed to be united ... There is the Jewish people, and this is a Jewish nation-state that has also an Arab minority (Official 11).

Official 11, like many of the other Jewish officials, is caught between commitment to Zionist ideas such as the importance of the unity of the Jewish people and values such as equality.

Finally, the Arab officials I interviewed, although accepting the definition of Israel as Jewish and democratic and its centrality to Citizenship Education in Israel, were aware of the marginalised position ascribed to the Palestinian minority by this hegemonic discourse:

> In one of the discussions we talked about identity and recognising the other and someone very senior among the committee members told me: look, if you won't accept my existence as Zionist I will find it very difficult to accept your otherness. My answer was simple: if you'll tell me what is my place in your identity I won't have any problem accepting you as a Zionist. This was my answer and this is why I think that in this question it is not in my hands (Official 13).

Official 13 draws our attention to the fact that the supposed inclusivity of the new Citizenship Curriculum does not necessarily mean that the Palestinian minority are included within the concept of Israeli citizenship. For Official 13, as long as the basis for Citizenship Education is the state of Israel as Jewish and democratic, Palestinian students will be marginalised. For the Arab officials, the great challenge as educators (which largely remained unanswered) was how to reconcile their aspirations to educate their students towards democratic, active and involved citizenship with the exclusions they experience.

Conclusions

Three types of discourse can be identified from the analysis presented in this chapter: 1) those which construct the link between nationality and citizenship as universal, using liberal-democratic language and drawing upon the image of 'a nation with a right for a state'; 2) those which construct citizenship status as derived from national belonging, seeing the link between Jewish nationality and Israeli citizenship as unique; and 3) those articulated by the Arab officials which might be interpreted as an attempt to resist the dominant discourse. In doing so, Arab officials suggested that the Jewish-Zionist discourse, with its strong connection between nationhood and citizenship, could be used as a platform for engaging Arab students in a discussion about their own national identity.

Nevertheless, despite the different views presented by the officials, and despite the fact that the Arab officials' responses could to some extent be interpreted as a form of resistance, all the officials in this study constructed the aims of Citizenship Education in Israel within the framework of the hegemonic discourse. The myth of Israel as a Jewish and democratic state with a Jewish identity remained unchallenged, despite its exclusionary implications.

To a significant extent, the discourse of inclusivity in the curriculum guidelines was not maintained when the officials dealt with the desirable definition of Israeli citizenship, the sort of belonging it is supposed to generate, and especially with the ways in which it constructs the Other. Wittingly or unwittingly, this perpetuates the differential structure of Israeli citizenship and the tensions emerging from it. Perhaps the main question we ought to ask ourselves is whether it is possible to offer an inclusive Citizenship Education without challenging the myth of Israeli citizenship. In the light of the tensions and contradictions discussed in this chapter it might be argued that even 'progressive' Citizenship Education can only be seen as the first step along a very long road.

References

Abu-Asba, K (1997) *The Arab School System in Israel: Status Quo and Alternative Structure*. Givat Haviva: Givat Haviva Centre for Peace Research (Hebrew)

Al-Haj, M (1994) *The Arab School System in Israel: Issues and Trends*. Jerusalem: Flocehaimer Institution for Policy Research (Hebrew)

Beck, J (1998) *Morality and Citizenship in Education*. London: Cassell

Billing, M (1995) *Banal Nationalism*. London: Saga Publications

Carr, W (1991) Education for citizenship, in: *British Journal of Education Studies*, 39(4): 373-385

Davies, I, Gregory, I and Riley, C (1999) *Good Citizenship and Educational Provision*. London: Falmer Press

Derricott, R (1998) National case studies of citizenship education, in: Cogan, J J and Derricott, R (eds) *Citizenship for the 21st Century*. London: Kogan Page

Dussel, I, Tiramonti, G and Birgin, A (2000) Decentralisation and Recentralisation in the Argentine Educational reform, in: Popkewitz, T S (ed) *Educational Knowledge: Changing relationships between the state, civil society and the educational community*. Albany: State University of New York

Evans, K M (1998) *Shaping Futures: Learning for competence and citizenship*. Aldershot: Ashgate

Kennedy, K J (1997) Citizenship education in review: past perspectives and future needs, in: Kennedy, K J (ed) *Citizenship Education and the Modern State*. London: Falmer Press

Kimmerling, B (2001) *The Invention and Decline of Israeliness: State, society and the military.* Berkeley: University of California Press

Laclau, E and Mouffe, C (2001) (2nd edition) *Hegemony and Socialist Strategy: Towards a radical democratic politics.* London: Verso

Lemish, P (2003) Civic and citizenship education in Israel, in: *Cambridge Journal of Education,* 33(1): 53-72

McLaughlin, T H (1992) Citizenship, diversity and education; a philosophical perspective, in: *Journal of Moral Education,* 22(3): 235-250

Ministry of Education (Curriculum Department) (1994) *Citizenship Education: Curriculum guidelines for high schools in the Jewish sector (state schools and state religious schools), the Arab sector and the Druze sector.* Jerusalem: Ministry of Education (Hebrew)

Ministry of Education (2000a) *To Be Citizens in Israel: A Jewish and Democratic State.* Jerusalem: Ministry of Education (Hebrew)

Ministry of Education (2000b) *The General Manager Guidelines,* no. 7:1. Jerusalem: Ministry of Education (Hebrew)

Ministry of Education (2001) *The General Manager Guidelines,* no. 7:1. Jerusalem: Ministry of Education (Hebrew)

Pearce, N and Hallgarten J (2000) Introduction, in: Pearce, N and Hallgarten, J (eds) *Tomorrow's Citizens: Critical debates in citizenship and education.* London: Institute for Public Policy Research

Pinson, H (2000) The Role of Citizenship Education in a Multicultural Society and a Nation-Building State. Unpublished M.Phil thesis: University of Cambridge

Popkewitz, T S (2000) Globalisation/regionalisation, knowledge, and educational practice: some notes on comparative strategies for educational research, in: Popkewitz, T S (ed) *Educational Knowledge: changing relationships between the state, civil society and the educational community.* Albany: State University of New York

Popkewitz, T S and Brennan, M (1998) Restructuring social and political theory in education: Foucault and the social epistemology of school practices, in: Popkewitz, T S and Brennan, M (eds) *Foucault's Challenge: Discourse, knowledge, and power in education.* New York: Teachers College Press

Resnik, J (1999) Particularistic versus universalistic content in the Israeli education system, in: *Curriculum Inquiry,* 29(4): 485-511

Shafir, G and Peled, Y (2002) *Being Israeli.* Cambridge: Cambridge University Press

8

The tragedy of peace education, and its transformation

JEAN McNIFF

In this chapter, Jean McNiff argues for a peace education which is grounded both in intellectual and social freedom and in the recognition of opposition and conflict. Without an understanding of the agonistic nature of human relations, she argues, peace education is nothing more than an artificial smoothing over of irreconcilable differences, and a perpetuation of existing practices of colonisation, oppression and control. McNiff's thesis is that real peace-making needs to be based on the recognition that not all human beliefs and values are commensurable or reconcilable, and that contradiction and conflict are not pathologies, but essential characteristics both of humanity and of the learning process. There is a powerful link here between the recognition of differences of culture and perspective described by Bond, Panjwani and Pinson and the proposals McNiff puts forward for viewing these conflicts as an integral part of the peace education process.

Introduction

Since I delivered an earlier version of this paper, entitled 'The tragedy of peace education', at the second Discourse Power Resistance Conference in April 2003, I have thought much about the paper and its title; and in this chapter, I develop both in the light of my reflections. While I still hold with the basic premises of the original (McNiff, 2003a), I do not think that the ideas and title went far enough. I still believe, as I argued in the original, that conceptualisations and practices of peace education appear to be grounded in tragedy, on two counts, as I shall shortly explain. However, given my unceasing commitment to generative transformational processes (see McNiff, 2000, 2002), I have come to understand that tragedy itself can be avoided, and that seemingly destructive contexts can, by the exercise of political will, be transformed into contexts for universal life-affirming practices. This chapter therefore aims to set out my understanding of how and why peace education, if its aims are to promote peaceful practices, needs to be seen as a process that aims to transform practices that are currently grounded in epistemological and social domination and oppression into practices of intellectual and social freedom. Without intellectual freedom, social freedom is unattainable, and without social freedom, peace is a mirage. I believe that a peace that is premised on the overt or subtle manipulation of minds, a coercive process that aims to persuade people that they are free, is no peace at all but the most egregious form of personal and social terrorism.

What I am saying here is coloured by my writing context. I am writing in South Africa, a country that appears to have achieved its own miracle of massive social and political change. This has happened at speed, and without a blood bath as was feared in the early 1990s. What is happening here, I believe, gives hope for the future. South Africa has shown that, provided the political will is there, it is possible for a previously war-torn people to stop the killing. Of course deep problems remain. Many die-harders resist the new dispensations. Many have left the country, rather than accept the new conditions. Yet many seem determined to build a new future, a new country, and to transform old traditions into new beginnings (Said, 1975). It is hard all round for people to find a middle ground, particularly in light of the emergence of new forms of social injustice. Many people I meet, while acknowledging the benefits of the new, still shaky stability, raise questions about whether the peace will last because although new political structures are in place to ensure that all people and their contributions may be valued, the enactment of those policies carries its own new potentials for social injustice. This is a familiar story. Revolution, Hannah Arendt (1990) tells us, always embeds its own conditions for violence. Yet this has become a core element in my own understanding. I have come to understand that recognition of the potentials for violence is a necessary condition for peace. It is by recognising the potentials for violence within the conditions of peace, and working them into conditions of non-violence, that the idea of peace actually makes practical sense. It is out of this understanding that I write because from my position as an educational researcher, dominant forms of peace research and peace education, which are supposed to encourage peaceful social practices, and which appear most elegant on paper, do not actually offer realistic conceptual frameworks for real-life processes of social change. They do not re-cognise the fragility and volatility of life and relationships, but assume that people are a homogenous group who will behave in accordance with a given rhetoric and in terms of a given theoretical framework. To me, this does not make sense. My understanding of social living is that we are all different and have different values perspectives, which need to be recognised and respected. Like Berlin (1997) I believe that we are all gloriously imperfect, that our quarrels are an integral part of our interactions, and that our peaceful relationships are grounded in our capacity to turn our quarrels into mutually negotiated forms of living, without compromise of personal dignity or infringement of personal freedom. Given this commitment to the inevitably contra-dictory nature of human living, I wonder what would it take for Kant's idea of perpetual peace (1970) to be realised at a practical level? What would it take to understand peace at a theoretical level so that forms of peace research and peace education really would have significance for the realisation of peaceful practices? These are the issues I would like to explore here.

To set the scene, I want to see how conceptualisations of peace educa-tion might be inherently tragic on two counts: first, in the sense that peace needs to be understood as an experience that is grounded in contradiction, and second that, many people active in peace education are working from inappropriate perspectives, which is a tragic state of affairs. I also want to stay with my consistent metaphor of generative transformational potentials, and explain my understanding of how peace can emerge from violence, and how peace education itself can be transformed. To make sense of all this, I need to explain my under-standing of the nature of tragedy.

The nature of tragedy

In a *Times Higher Education Supplement* article (2002), Ken Hirschkop comments on the responses of Americans to the Twin Towers disaster in 2001. He says that many speak about the event as a national tragedy. The event is generally viewed, rightly, in Hirschkop's opinion, as an experience of untold pain and suffering, whose occurrence has profound implications for the American public. It should not, however, be regarded as a tragedy. Atrocity, yes. Devastation and horrendous misery, yes. Tragedy, no. The irony for Hirschkop is that, while many Americans react with horror and disbelief that someone could do such a thing to them, many also react with horror and disbelief to the suggestion that there might be reasons other than 'sheer, inexplicable malignity' (p. II) for its perpetration. This seeming inability by some to comprehend the catastrophe in political terms, suggests Hirschkop, is rooted partly in the lack of a tragic dimension in American popular culture. It is not, he says, that American culture avoids disasters or calamities; it is more that these are not understood in political terms, and are therefore inappropriately construed as tragic.

This raises questions about how tragedy is understood. While many interpretations of tragedy exist, it is generally agreed that tragedy is not just the occurrence of disasters such as plane crashes and earthquakes

> whatever definition is chosen, tragedy in its modern form depends on plots in which good intentions, or competing but valid priorities, are deflected or channeled towards unexpected outcomes. Tragic suffering is not inflicted by simple villainy: it represents the working-out of a complex action, in which the motives and deeds of characters often contribute to unforeseen and unintended misery. The eventual disaster stems from a sequence of events, and is sometimes the direct consequence of the actions (Macbeth) or the inaction (Hamlet) of the victim. As the complex results of an intersection of actions and motives, tragedies, even when they have distinct villains (Iago, for instance), can therefore entail an interesting degree of moral ambiguity. (Hirschkop, 2002: 2)

This insight is instructive for an understanding of peace education. My own experience of working in politically contested contexts such as Northern Ireland, Palestine and Israel, and now South Africa, is that many situations are not only characterised by violence, which can lead to personal and social disasters, but are also inherently tragic, in that the lives of so many well-intentioned citizens, both those who simply want to get on with their lives as well as those who are actively working for peace, are caught up in violent politically constituted struggles with which they disagree. This process distorts their lives and their capacity to live peacefully with their neighbours, as shown in *The Observer*, 2003 report on the penalties facing conscientious objectors in Israel. Many have to fight to protect themselves, often at the expense of their own values of peace, freedom and justice for all. Indeed, peace building itself often manifests as a violent process (Mallie and McKittrick, 2001).

It is a characteristic of tragedy that it is always enacted at the level of human life-world experience, not at the level of systemic structures and processes. When tragedy happens, it is often because of the seemingly irreconcilable tensions between the individual or collective and the system, either because the system constitutes the embedding context for the individual or collective, who therefore find themselves in conflict with others; or because the individual or collective has come to accept the norms of the system, often in spite of their own values base, and therefore causes conflict. It is often a case of a conflict of narratives, visions and values, as these translate into actions: the individual narratives of citizens who wish to find a way through, so that all members of the community may live in peace, against the grand policy narratives that maintain the discourses of division through domination and control. The tragedy of many conflicts is that while the problems might be intractable and reconciliation might only as yet be a vision because of the enormous complexity of claims and counter-claims, those who do wish to find spaces for negotiated living in their historically and politically constituted contexts are systematically prevented from doing so, both by the official canons and also by the inexorable tit-for-tat that is a feature of the ongoing violent situation. In many instances, living with the violence, and perpetrating violence as a means of self protection or as a means of expressing moral outrage against existing injustices, constitutes the deepest tragedy for those whose goals are social justice and freedom for all.

The tragedy of dominant conceptualisations of peace education

I am concerned that dominant conceptualisations of peace education appear not to be premised on values widely believed to contribute to social practices that act in everyone's interests. The values in question are to do with freedom, justice, universal suffrage, and the reasonably fair and equitable distribution of social goods among all members of a community. Processes of peacemaking are popularly believed to be premised on the ideas of equal representation for all, and a form of democracy that ensures public participation in policy debates, especially about the kind of society people wish to live in. The literatures of peace education and peacemaking largely endorse these ideas.

A close look at how those values might be realised in practice reveals some slippage. The values underpinning dominant forms of peace education seem to be more to do with colonisation, oppression and control than to do with freedom for all and living according to one's chosen plans. The dominant methodologies of peace education, and their realisation in practice, appear to be more to do with the concentration of privilege in the hands of already dominant groupings than with efforts to ensure the conditions of justice for all, through the establishment of appropriate social infrastructures. In the cases of many contexts of political and geographical dispute, such as Northern Ireland and the Middle East, the hidden message is that communities can have peace provided Party A agrees to conform to what Party B wishes them to do (de Bréadún, 2001; Said, 2002. This message is illustrated in archive footage I saw in Johannesburg's Apartheid Museum, where Nelson Mandela refused the original terms for peace on the grounds that the kind of peace on offer would be no peace at all. This tendency is not confined to any one side but is evident everywhere. Self-interest involving compliance by the other seems to have become an unquestioned, almost normative, stance. While this arrangement might lead to a situation of no war for both parties, and might be the kind of peaceful situation that Party A wants, it is far removed from the aspirations of what Party B would wish for themselves. The hidden assumption is that Party B can have peace provided its members relinquish their claims to independence of mind, spirit and body, and by implication land and identity, and surrender their capacity for free thinking and action and the formation of their own life plans to a dominant authority. Given this set of terms and conditions, it is hardly surprising that many minority communities refuse to accept the form of peace on offer, and continue to resist, often at the cost of their own lives. Given these terms and conditions, many forms of peace education appear as forms of colonisation and control, dressed up nicely in the rhetoric of freedom and independence.

This situation denies my own values of freedom and fairness. I believe that peace education needs to be taken very seriously indeed, because it offers important political and ideological frameworks for the kinds of social practices endorsed at policy level and worked towards by communities through the social institutions of formal schooling and political debate. It is anticipated that the assumptions underpinning peace education will eventually become structured into systemic discourses and practices. If those assumptions are themselves grounded in premises whose realisation is contradictory to its espoused values, peace education will instead promote social practices that are anything but peaceful.

Instead, peace education needs to be grounded in the practicalities of life experiences, in the contradictory, volatile and problematic nature of human living. I want to make a case for the agonistic foundations of peace. The idea of agonistics, derived from the Greek *agon*, is to do with tragedy, a concept that people's good intentions can be caught up in forces outside their control and diverted and distorted into outcomes they never originally intended. It refers to the tensions experienced when personal and social values are contradicted by internal or external forces, many of which deny the realisation of those values (Whitehead, 1989, 2000; Hamilton, 2002). Above all, it deals with the idea of moral ambiguity, especially in the face of the understanding that not all human beliefs and values are commensurable or reconcilable (Berlin, 2002).

Most current forms of peace education do not recognise the agonistic, contradictory base of human living, much of which manifests as conflict. Too often current forms are animated by assumptions about the rightness of what is known and the rightness of who knows it, about the unambiguous moral positioning of all participants, and about the certainty of concrete situations. It is assumed that someone is right and someone is wrong, that someone is legitimated in claiming the moral high ground, as if there is one form of morality to which every-one subscribes. It is also assumed that arguments are to do with right and wrong, not to do with competing rights, or with a willingness to engage in public debates about the justification of moral and political stances, and that problems can be brought to closure. These assump-tions do not engage with the realities of human experience, namely that human experience is to do with conflicting claims for rights and goods, and each one of those claims should be understood as legiti-mate on its own terms. Nor is there a moral high ground that is recog-nised as such by all. What is moral for one is not necessarily moral for another, nor is there a universal set of standards by which to deter-mine whose morality is the right one for all. To assume that issues of moral ambiguity are resolvable by an appeal to the dominant canons of any one culture is to impose a set of parameters on the concept of peace that threatens to turn peace education into a grand narrative of dominance and oppression. To assume that moral ambiguity is resolv-able in the first place is to strip human experience of its tragic nature and reduce it to the level of skilful performance and to reduce peace education to a tragedy in form and content, with no hope for trans-formation. Peace education, a field whose underpinning philosophies should be informed by the highest principles of human well-being, is itself distorted into a form of terrorism when the values of freedom and the truths of multiple ways of living are shoe-horned into culturally-specific ways of being.

The transformative nature of peace education

I want to make a case for a form of peace education premised on the agonistic base of human experience, and grounded in the trans-formative nature of educative relationships. I hope to demonstrate my commitment to trying to work towards a value system that fully accepts the crooked nature of my own and other people's humanity (Berlin, 1990), yet fully commits to taking responsibility for trans-forming potentially destructive relationships into life-affirming ones, through individual and collective political will.

Human living is characterised by contradiction and conflict. These are not pathologies. They are the experiences of daily living. Indeed, contradiction and conflict are essential for maintaining an open stance to on-going learning (McNiff, 2003b). Peace education has to engage with the ideas of contradiction, that values are frequently denied in practice, and that people have to work long and hard in order to aspire to those values, which are often in conflict. One person's deeply held value of freedom is often contradicted by their equally deeply held value of social justice. Justice and freedom are in many ways incommensurable. I cannot exercise my freedom to do as I please without jeopardising the freedom of others to do as they please. Exercising my freedom to drive my big car diminishes other people's freedom to enjoy clean air, or their freedom to conserve limited environmental resources. We cannot have it all ways. Sadly, many forms of peace education are premised on the idea that we can. This view needs to be transformed. Rather than work from the assumption that values are always commensurate at an individual and collective level, and that conflicts can and should be resolved, peace education needs instead to take as its starting point the reality of frequently irreconcilable moral ambiguities and competing rights claims. It needs to recognise the inherently tragic nature of human living, to rescue itself from becoming a superficial narrative about overcoming disasters and glossing over human frailty, and become a critically-engaged context for the expression of the deepest compassion for self and others as the basis for working towards universal freedom and social justice.

The peace that peace education is striving to secure should not be conceptualised as a static form of experience. Peaceful practices, like all practices, contain their own transformative potentials for new forms of an unanticipated nature. One practice changes into another, rapidly and unpredictably, because of the shifting nature of the relationships and interests of participants. What appears to be a loving relationship at one moment can rapidly turn into jealousy and rage in the next, rage can turn into understanding and quietude. Human relationships are seldom static, because humans are always in the process of development in relation to themselves, and to one another.

So what price Kant's idea of perpetual peace? The idea cannot make sense if peace is conceptualised as a static state to be aimed for on some distant horizon. It can make sense if peace is conceptualised as a form of living rooted in an understanding that all human experience is inherently volatile, and that lasting stability needs to be worked at.

Peace is not an institution that can be manufactured by policy makers. It is a practice that exists in the relationships among people. Peace is not a thing or a place. It is a human practice whose nature is realised through the practice. Peace does not come into existence in spite of the struggle, but because of the struggle, and it embeds its own inherent potential to transform into different versions of itself. How those versions manifest themselves is down to the political will of real people. If we wish, we can all secure the conditions of peace by trying to reach a deeper understanding about the conditions for justice and ensuring that those conditions are realised (Young, 1990). We can obstruct the conditions of peace by refusing to listen to other narratives, and pursuing our own self interests. Peace is not a static state that once achieved becomes the norm. Peace is potentially the grounds for violence, in the same way that violence is potentially the grounds for peace. People and their life situations are always in dialectical tension, driven as we are by different values and interests, and by our dispositions for destructive tendencies as well as for life-affirming ones (Alford, 1997).

Transforming the rhetoric into practice

It came as something of a surprise to me when my work began to be positioned within the discourses of peace education. As far as I was concerned, my work was to do with enabling educators to understand and improve their practice. The animating principle was that educators would ask, 'How do I improve what I am doing?' (Whitehead, 1989, 2000), and undertake their action research to generate validated evidence in support of any claims that they had indeed improved their work. This involved holding themselves accountable for their educative influence in the lives of others. Over time, and working from this perspective, significant numbers of educators have been awarded their masters and doctoral degrees for studying and evaluating their own practice (see for example, Cahill, 2000; McDonagh, 2000; Roche, 2000; Sullivan, 2000). I eventually came to see the links being made at a substantive level, in terms of the relationship between specific contexts of my work and peace education. (McNiff, McGeady and Elliott, 2001) which is a research report about working with educators in Northern Ireland in the curriculum strand entitled *Education for Mutual Understanding*).

However, I remained vaguely dissatisfied with this state of affairs. Something quite fundamental was eluding me. I clearly experienced myself as the living contradiction Jack Whitehead (2003) speaks about, in that my values were not being realised in practice. My understanding was that my work was about creating the kinds of relationships and contexts that encourage processes of learning, not as some perceived, to do with substantive issues. That tension is beginning to be resolved. By living and working with the contradiction I am now beginning to understand and develop it in a way that seems right for me.

The significance of the work should not be seen as located within a subject matter or specific context. The fact that I worked with a small number of teachers in troubled Northern Ireland was possibly more dramatic in public perceptions than the fact that I worked with hundreds of teachers just down the road in the Republic. Yet the methodological orientation was the same. The vague feeling of contradiction became crystallised into a deeper understanding both of my work and of how public perceptions around peace education come to be shaped. It was easy enough to make the links between subject matters such as Education for Mutual Understanding and peace education at a substantive level, yet this rather facile link was a manifestation of simplistic popular conceptualisation of peace as a state to be aimed for which, once achieved, will then endure of its own momentum. On the contrary, I do not see a context of geographical-political violence as a more noteworthy context for peace making than the circumstances of everyday life, other than for its dramatic impact. Trying to establish the validity and legitimacy of practitioner action research within higher education institutional settings in the battle for ideas can be every bit as politically constituted and potentially destructive as the difficulties educators face when trying to transform their contexts of violent battles for land and civil rights. Lyotard (1986) is right to talk of intellectual terrorism in the academy. Bourdieu (1988) is right to speak of the violence of institutional practices that require intellectual subservience as a prerequisite to organisational survival. My work directly challenged the ideas of subservience and the practices of domination and oppression. I was encouraging workplace-based practitioners to see their research accounts as valuable contributions to public bodies of knowledge, and to see themselves as knowledge workers whose living educational theories (Whitehead, 1989), grounded in their educative relationships, were every bit as legitimate as the more conceptual theories of many higher education workers. By sticking with my vague sense of dissatisfaction at the tendency of others to remain with a subject orientation, I came gradually to understand that the methodological frameworks I had chosen to work by were actually enabling me to conceptualise peace as a living process, is grounded in a dogged determination to resist the imposition of unjustifiable forms of intellectual control, to refuse to be colonised, and to transform social conditions that perpetuate practices of domination and oppression into practices of respect and recognition of all. Like Nigel Mellor (1998), I came to see that the struggle *was* the methodology.

My current understanding is that the methodology is the peace process. Peace processes are about people trying to reach common ground with their neighbours, even when both parties are in quite fundamental disagreement with each other and wish to remain so. The methodologies of peace processes are about adopting a critical stance to one's own positioning, so that although one makes claims to new knowledge, one always holds that knowledge provisionally, and admits the possibility that one can transform current learning by learning more.

The literature and practice of practitioner action research are therefore directly linked with the literature and practice of peace education. Educational work is a form of social activism, a practice rooted in the capacity of collectives of individuals to think for themselves rather than be passive consumers of other people's knowledge (Russell, 1932). Many public accounts show how the critical perspectives adopted within their action enquiries have enabled practitioners to generate significant social change by transforming existing systemic structures and procedures into living forms of life-affirming relationships (Moira Laidlaw, Paul Murray and Margaret Farren: see reference list for website addresses). These accounts demonstrate the commitments of educators to take responsibility for their work as they strive to transform previously oppressive social structures and processes to celebrate a commitment to the uniqueness and creative capacity of every individual.

Transforming tragedy

The potential for tragedy has to be recognised as an inalienable property of human living, which can be avoided, provided the political will is there. Social living is not easy. As I write in South Africa, I know that many people would rather things were back as they used to be prior to 1994, when the new government came into power. I know that many people find compromise terribly difficult. I also know that huge goodwill drives many people, who are deeply committed to building a new country and a new future.

Building sustainable futures can be greatly assisted through formal education systems, provided they are animated by the principles of values pluralism and pluralistic freedom. More than ever I am convinced of the inextricably intertwined nature of the interrelationships between social and epistemological systems. How we live is informed by how we think. How students come to live can be influenced by how their teachers act; and how teachers act is influenced by how they think. Teachers need to be sure of their own capacity to build educative relationships grounded in their own and others' freedom to choose, and be committed to taking responsibility for how they are with their students and colleagues.

And finally ...

I want to end by pointing to my own capacity to transform my practice through learning, by refusing to continue to experience myself as a living contradiction and determining to do something about it, whilst recognising that new contractions will arise out of the resolution. This chapter is itself a transformation of its previous version. If you compare the two, I hope you will share my understanding of how my own range has extended, how I have transformed my previous tendency to remain stuck in a negative discourse into one of a celebration of hope and a determination to bring the hope into practice. This is what I live to do. This is how I define my life in education.

References

Alford, C F (1997) *What Evil Means to Us*. Ithaca: Cornell University Press

Arendt, H (1990) *On Revolution*. London: Penguin

Berlin, I (1990) *The Crooked Timber of Humanity: Chapters in the history of ideas*. London: Fontana Press

Berlin, I (1997) *Against the Current: Essays in the history of ideas* (edited by H. Hardy). London: Pimlico

Berlin, I (2002) *Freedom and its Betrayal: Six enemies of human liberty* (edited by H. Hardy). London: Chatto and Windus

Bourdieu, P (1988) *Homo Academicus*. London: Polity Press

Cahill, M (2000) How can I Encourage Pupils to Participate in their Own Learning? Unpublished MA dissertation. Bristol: University of the West of England

De Bréadún, D (2001) *The Far Side of Revenge: Making Peace in Northern Ireland*. Cork: The Collins Press

Farren, M http://www.compapp.dcu.ie/~mfarren accessed 14th June 2003

Hamilton, M L (2002) Living our contradictions: caught between our words and our actions around social justice, in: *The School Field*, 12(3/4): 19-31

Hirschkop, K (2002) A nation in need of some real tragic characters, in: *The Times Higher Education Supplement*, December 20/27, page II in MLA Convention Section

Kant, I (1970) Toward perpetual peace: a philosophical sketch, in: Reiss, H (ed) *Kant's Political Writings*. Cambridge: Cambridge University Press

Laidlaw, M http://www.actionresearch.net/moira.shtml accessed 14th June 2003

Lyotard, J-F (1986) *The Postmodern Condition: A report on knowledge*. Manchester: Manchester University Press

Mallie, E and McKittrick, D (2001) *Endgame in Ireland*. London: Hodder and Stoughton

McDonagh, C (2000) Towards a Theory of a Professional Teacher Voice: How can I improve my teaching of pupils with specific learning difficulties in the area of language? Unpublished MA dissertation. Bristol: University of the West of England. Available at http://www.jeanmcniff.com/dissertations

McNiff, J with Whitehead, J (2000) *Action Research in Organisations*. London: Routledge

McNiff, J with Whitehead, J (2002) (2nd edn) *Action Research: Principles and Practice*. London: RoutledgeFalmer

McNiff, J (2003a) The tragedy of peace education. Paper presented at the second Discourse Power Resistance Conference, University of Plymouth, UK, April, available at htttp://www.jeanmcniff.com/writings

McNiff, J (2003b) Peace education and other stories of violence. Paper presented at an invitational seminar, Ben Gurion University of the Negev, Beer Sheva. Available at http://www.jeanmcniff.com/papersforisrael

McNiff, J, McGeady, L and Elliott, M R (2001) Time to Listen. Evaluation report for the Project 'Time to Listen', Portadown. Available at http://www.jeanmcniff.com/timetolisten

Mellor, N (1998) Notes from a method, in: *Educational Action Research*, 6(3): 453-470

Murray, P http://www.royagcol.ac.uk/%7Epaul_murray/Sub_Pages/Further Information.htm accessed 14th June 2003

Roche, M (2000) How can I Improve my Practice so as to Help my Pupils to Philosophise? Unpublished MA dissertation. Bristol: University of the West of England. Available at http://www.jeanmcniff.com/dissertations

Russell, B (1932) *Education and the Social Order.* London: Routledge and Kegan Paul

Said, E (1975) *Beginnings: Intention and Method.* New York: Basic Books

Said, E (2002) (2nd edn) *The End of the Peace Process.* London: Granta

Sullivan, B (2000) How can I Help my Pupils to Make more Effective Use of their Time in School? Unpublished MA dissertation. Bristol: University of the West of England

The Observer (2003) Netanyahu nephew faces jail as army refusnik, 9th March, p7

Whitehead, J (1989) Creating a living educational theory from questions of the kind, 'How do I improve my practice?', in: *Cambridge Journal of Education,* 19(1): 137-153

Whitehead, J (2000) How do I improve my practice? Creating and legitimating an epistemology of practice, in: *Reflective Practice,* 1(1): 91-104

Whitehead, J (2003) Ubuntu, the loving eye of an ecological feminism, post-colonial practice and influencing the education of social formations, http://www.actionresearch.net/writings/jw17nov03.htm Accessed 15th November 2003

Young, I M (1990) *Justice and the Politics of Difference.* Princeton, NJ: Princeton University Press

PART THREE
IMAGES, VISION

9

Learning in the clouds: what can be learned about the unknowable?

JEROME SATTERTHWAITE

Jerome Satterthwaite returns in this chapter to the radical questions about knowledge and learning: What can we know? How do we learn? He argues for a recovery of the sense of strangeness which goes with the recognition that to gain knowledge may not be the only, or indeed the most powerfully motivating, goal of learning. There is what lies beyond knowledge; and by dint of strenuous effort we can be brought to an encounter with that strangeness. This chapter resonates well with the argument put forward by Ecclestone in volume two of this series, and contributes to the defamiliarisation of conventional education theory and practice which is the shared project of the authors in this section.

Strangeness, difference, otherness – being not like us, not like me! There is discomfort here: it is comfortable to be akin. What is not akin to me is not kind – not my kind – and I shrink from it. An easy way to reassure myself about these feelings is to couple the notion of strangeness to a sense of disapproval: strangeness becomes improper, suspect, perhaps indecorous, indecent. It will be an easy step to take from here, to move to the stance of disdain, holding that strangeness is contemptible.

That there is strangeness in our world is a view easily ridiculed by the intellectual stance we call enlightenment, famously exemplified in Hume, whose perfect scepticism allowed him the rejoinder to any and every strange thing that it was merely a matter of fact for which the explanation was so far not apparent. Logical positivism, as expounded by the likes of Bertrand Russell, took the next and final step to complete the banishment of strangeness from our discourse, insisting that statements for which evidence could not be adduced were neither true nor false, but meaningless. Strangeness henceforth became a characteristic of discourses such as poetry, myth, fairy tale, religion: fanciful, empty of meaning. Yet, doggedly, people persist in wanting to encounter strangeness: to learn things so strange that they cannot be known, still less spoken of.

What makes people want to learn things they know they cannot know? Is it something akin to Shelley's *desire of the moth for the star* (Shelley, 1977:164)? Do people want to learn about the unknowable in protest against the dreariness of what can be known? Is it boredom, world-weariness; or the recognition that although minds are limited, what lies beyond knowledge is no less real and no less fascinating merely because it is beyond our intellectual grasp? Conversely, is it because we are realists, or in the grip of a dismal intellectual pessimism, that this comment of Robert Louis Stevenson (Stevenson, 1881) seems so dated? *We are so constituted that our hopes are inaccessible, like stars, and the term of hoping is prolonged until the term of life... to travel hopefully is a better thing than to arrive.*

Put another way, what are we resisting if we direct our gaze, in the words of Faber's hymn of 1854, *Out beyond the shining of the furthest star?* Is this something we should be encouraged to do, or is this merely escapism? These questions betray my defensiveness, my anxiety that this chapter may seem perverse in a work focused on contemporary issues of discourse, power and resistance in education: this chapter is just about to put its head in the clouds. I have chosen two clouds, two regions of impenetrable darkness: the *Cloud of Unknowing* of 14th Century English mysticism, and the black hole of contemporary astrophysics. I want to investigate two darknesses where contemporary educational politics is insignificant, in the hope of learning something about education from the strangeness we encounter there.

Fourteenth Century English mysticism is strange but also strangely down to earth. When we look at the English mystics of the 14th Century we find men and women taking responsibility for their learn-

136

ing, and struggling, over a period of many years, to train themselves in the skills of a demanding discipline. They differ in many respects but one thing they share is a strenuous commitment to learning the hard way. Paradoxically, they insist both that the blessedness of their insight is a gift they could not earn, and that there is no substitute for the rigorous training which alone prepared them to receive it. Similarly, getting to understand the physics of black holes is an ordeal. Stephen Hawking, that most generous of men, promises (Hawking, 1995:ix) to give us this knowledge for £7.99, assuring us that *the basic ideas about the origin and fate of the universe can be stated without mathematics in a form that people without a scientific education can understand.* He is wrong. The path before the student of astrophysics is beset with mathematics of the weirdest and most intimidating difficulty, as the vehicle for an argument which proceeds, step by step, with ever increasing complexity, to 'unweave a rainbow', as Keats put it, rendering an account of the universe at once prosaic and exotic in the extreme. The mind is stupefied in trying to grapple with this matter of fact account of the unimaginable.

Controversial conclusions emerge from this enquiry. Firstly, we are disconcerted to find that student-centredness, or at least one understanding of that well worn phrase, has no place in either of the disciplines we are concerned with. Neither the mystic nor the astrophysicist is patient with the requirement that our needs as students should be met, our individual learning styles respected, our personal agendas taken into account. What matters to them is what is encountered rather than anything about the learner who comes to that encounter: the object rather than the subject. The mystics and the astrophysicists are in agreement that there is delight to be had and that the learning is dazzlingly rewarded but they also insist that personal concerns are to be set aside as interference. Secondly, we are brought to recognise that there is little scope here for learning from experience, which has nothing to teach us that can help us on our way. Indeed, both disciplines insist that much of what we have experienced will have furnished us with preconceptions we must learn to set aside, since they prevent our understanding. Thirdly, and perhaps most disconcertingly, we are confronted in these disciplines with élitism: it appears that these learning objectives are attainable only for a chosen few. We need to look at how those few are chosen, who chooses them, and what happens about the rest of us. Finally, we are faced with an issue about curriculum: what sort of learning is this and what is the point of pursuing it these days?

Here is the author of *The Cloud of Unknowing* (*Cloud*, 1964:15), telling us how to approach God:

> And therefore I would leave all that thing that I can think. For why, he may well be loved, but not thought. By love may he be gotten and holden; but by thought neither. And therefore, although it be good sometime to think... nevertheless in this work it shall be cast down and covered with a *cloud of forgetting*. And thou shalt step above it stalwartly, but listily, with a devout and pleasing stirring of love, and try to pierce that darkness above thee. And smite upon that thick *cloud of unknowing* with a sharp dart of longing love; and go not thence for aught that befalleth.

'Although it be good sometime to think', as the author grudgingly concedes, we are being told here that in the work of contemplation everything we know as the result of thinking will clutter up our minds and get in the way of authentic learning, which is founded not in reason but in desire. Desire, the mystics insist, is all we need; wanting is everything. Conversely, every *thing* is, or should be, wanting, in the sense of being absent. This absolute requirement reminds us of perhaps the most obvious and most easily ignored of all the insights of the teaching profession, that people learn what they themselves want to learn, and learn little else. For the mystic, this is absolute. Nothing else matters: no questions about the ability of learner, in this case the contemplative, or about her or his intelligence, are of any significance. What matters is the extent, the depth and intensity of her or his desire. Mysticism is about longing, about the acknowledgement of need. This insight is central to education theory: before anything useful can happen, I must recognise my need to learn. Not how urgently I need to learn, but the extent to which I recognise and acknowledge that need, is what determines the benefit I gain. Mysticism shares with education and other branches of the study of minds the recognition that it is only what people themselves want that they have a chance of getting. We discover from the mystics the homely truth that it is impossible to teach people what they do not want to learn, or to give them what they do not want to receive. In the process of arriving at this recognition, we find we have smuggled back into the mystic's project something to do with the learner after all: the learner must be famished with desire to learn.

Thus far there is common ground between the mystic and the educational theorist. But we need to confront a second and more controversial point of comparison. The mystic's desire is the recognition of an absence. The learner is positioned as emptied of everything except desire, desire for what is absent and unknown. Self-awareness is ruled out; to be conscious of yourself is a cause for sorrow (*Cloud*:61).

> ...sit full still, as it were in a sleeping device, all forsobbed and forsunken in sorrow. This is true sorrow; this is perfect sorrow; and well were it with him that might win to this sorrow. All men have matter of sorrow; but most specially he feeleth matter of sorrow that knoweth and feeleth that he *is*.

This view of the learner, grieving over her or his self-awareness, seeking to press down beneath a cloud of forgetting even the fact of her or his own existence, is starkly at odds with received educational opinion. Perhaps ever since Plato, we have been discouraged from thinking of the learner as an empty vessel, waiting to be filled with the knowledge of the teacher. Learning has been understood to be a process of teasing out from and by the learners the insights and knowledges they already possess: a process of connecting the learners, their thoughts and experiences together with new knowledge which their ideas and experiences allow them to appropriate and make their own. The author of the *Cloud* will have none of this, insisting that to have a mind emptied of all preoccupations and preconceptions is the prerequisite of that encounter with deity, the absolute other, which is the aim of contemplation. Until we are emptied, even of self-awareness, we cannot be filled.

We are a long way here from received educational wisdom but the gap widens as we hear, this time from another 14th Century English mystic, Julian of Norwich, how it is that we come to desire, and why our desire will be satisfied. Her Lord says to her (Julian of Norwich, 1998:99)

> I am the foundation of your prayers: first it is my will that you should have something, and then I make you desire it, and then I make you pray for it, then how could it be that you should not have what you pray for?

Not only must this mystic empty herself, hollowed out in an attitude of simple desire, she learns that the source of that desire itself lies beyond and above her in the object which alone can satisfy it. It is her Lord who has made her need, and ask for, what he wishes to give her. The teacher of this mystic has emptied her of everything but desire so that she will yearn; he then satisfies her yearning by giving her what he has intended her to receive since time began. Stripped of everything to do with the self, knowing nothing, remembering nothing, turning away from the world of experience, purged of everything except desire, the mystic longs for that encounter with the strangeness which is at once the only satisfaction and the only source of that desire.

Mysticism, then, involves the mystic in a one-way traffic. Walter Hilton, a close contemporary of Julian of Norwich, makes this plain (Hilton, 1957:163):

> [God] implants this desire within you, and is Himself both the desire and the object of your desire... You yourself do nothing; you simply allow Him to work within your soul, accepting sincerely and gladly whatever He deigns to do in you.

Richard Rolle, writing earlier in the 14th Century, reinforces this point, insisting that the love the mystic experiences is put there by the God he loves (Rolle, 1992:25). He says to God

> You strip your lovers bare of all earthly things,
> Your powerful love invades them
> And, bursting forth in fire, they offer praises...

The mystic as passive, empty, ardently desiring: this is a model of the learner we have been taught to reject. There is something deeply troubling about the view, so wholeheartedly embraced by these writers, that their job is to wait for, or wait upon their Lord until he fills their hearts and minds with strange fire. A lecturer in education, stalking down the corridor to the next lecture with such a model of education in mind, in which the learners will be endlessly attentive, in attitudes of intense expectation, empty headed but yearning to be filled by her or his inspired outpourings, will have failed to grasp a fundamental axiom of education. We prefer the view that the student is in charge and already has the knowledge which our pedagogy merely helps to bring to light. But this is a view sharply at odds with the ardent posture of the mystic.

I turn now to another branch of learning where the journey's end is a similarly stunned aporia, comparable to the standstill to which the mystic is brought in the cloud of unknowing: I want to follow the argument (Cragg, 2003) which leads us to the knowledge of black holes. How do we arrive at a state of mind in which we can say that we understand the formation of a black hole? As we seek to answer this question we seem, at first sight, to have come across an approach to learning which is the polar opposite to the self-emptying kenosis of the mystic. We discover that we need a high level of mathematical competence: we must be able to follow an argument set out for the most part in algebraic equations, where most of the symbols will be the letters of the Greek alphabet, related by signs whose meaning must be taken on trust, as signifiers in a language without which the discussion cannot begin. Already we will have moved away from the world of experience to a world of concepts, whose relationship to the external world is conjectural, and appears to come and go, so that there will be stages in the reasoning where the equations are held to be descriptive of the external world, others where they are merely a rearrangement of symbols, allowing manipulations without which the argument cannot proceed. We shall see, as we follow the steps of the argument that leads us to posit the existence of black holes, how far we are removed from anything we can experience, and how reliant we are on theory, developed from a chain of reasoning derived to a very great extent from first principles: a procedure not unlike the dialectic of the theologian.

'Nature', James Jeans remarks, 'does not function in a way that can be made comprehensible to the human mind through models or pictures' (Jeans, 1981:10), hence the recourse to mathematics and striking parallel with mysticism. We are leaving behind the world of common sense and through procedures bearing comparison with those of the mystic outlined above, adopting an attitude of mind where immediate observation is impossible and misleading. We must rely on the powers of abstract reasoning, more or less imperfectly reinforced by indirect observations, themselves made possible and mediated through the deployment of instruments designed and built specifically to test the theories to which our speculative reasoning has given rise. Are astrophysicists rather like a sect, expressing their insights through a liturgy deeply significant amongst themselves, incomprehensible to the outsider?

141

At a level of advanced theoretical abstraction, we begin our enquiry into the formation of black holes by reasoning that small stars end their lives unremarkably: they merely fade away. But theory convinces us that stars with a greater mass are different. The matter they contain, according to the theory, cannot simply die away and cool to a motionless, dull silence; for larger stars their mass is sufficient to trigger a huge implosion called a Type II Supernova. This results in a shock wave that expels most of the star's envelope into space, as the core of the star collapses in on itself under gravity.

We have seen or directly experienced none of this. These events have never been witnessed. Indeed, if we were to observe events of this kind, we would, according to the theory, be gazing back millions of years in time, and be watching events unfolding not long after the world began in the present day. It is clear that what leads us so confidently to assert our grasp of the formation of a supernova cannot be a matter of trusting our senses, still less of trusting to that sturdy common sense by which we guide the choices we make from day to day. Yet it would be misleading to argue that claims of this kind are wholly without evidence to support them. Experiments from other areas of physics closer to home have been used to support theories about what happens to the core of a supernova. The results of these experiments are extrapolated to reinforce the argument that as the core collapses a density is reached where the core's electrons are pushed so tightly together that a new, outward pressure starts to become significant. This is electron degeneracy pressure which exerts a force that counteracts gravity and can stop the collapse. If the core is below a certain threshold mass, we reason that the collapse will be halted and equilibrium will be reached. A white dwarf results.

What have we learned and how have we learned it, if we halt the story here, content to have discovered the origins of a smallish star? The mystics empty their minds of all thought, memory, experience, ideas and concepts, and encounter an absolute in that darkness whose being they cannot doubt. By contrast, the process we are following relies on a chain of abstract reasoning, supported by the evidence of experiments nearer home, whose conclusions it is believed can be safely extrapolated, leading to claims beyond the reach of direct experience, which we trust because they are derived from laws whose operation is elsewhere in evidence. As an example of this process of reasoning, I quote from A.C. Phillips (Phillips, 2001:176):

> Chandrasekhar first deduced that there is a maximum value for the mass of a white dwarf in 1931. It was a momentous discovery.... [W]e shall see that this speculation has led to the conclusion that the other possible endpoints of stellar evolution are neutron stars and black holes.

The choice of words in this quotation is revealing: *deduced, discovery, speculation, conclusion*. Indeed, there is a pleasing ambiguity in the phrase *there is a maximum value for the mass of a white dwarf in 1931*. We are tempted to ask whether white dwarves are allowed a greater mass nowadays. They may be. Astrophysics moves on. Importantly, the stars in their courses also move on; they do what they do, whilst the astrophysicians' *deductions*, so easily and subtly modulated into *discoveries*, lead to *speculations* which then yield *conclusions* about them. Conclusions in logic are held to be the end of an argument. As the discussion advances towards this conclusion, we move to insights more and more remote from experience, beyond the reach of direct empirical support.

Two steps more in this argument take us to the black hole. As a first step, we consider the state of affairs where collapsing stellar cores are so massive that the outward pressure from degenerate electrons cannot support them. The inward flow continues and the proximity of the particles gets so extreme that they are forced to fuse together. Protons and electrons join to form neutrons. Now neutron degeneracy begins to play its part and exerts an outward force in a fresh attempt to regain equilibrium. If this neutron degeneracy pressure can halt the collapse, what remains is a neutron star. But what if even neutron degeneracy pressure fails to halt the collapse? The collapse of such a supermassive core has led it to achieve a density about which we can gain no information because at this point the collapsing star disappears. The core has become a black hole, and none of our theory and speculation can be tested on this new class of object, for it can give us no information. Nothing, not even light, escapes from a black hole. No empirical evidence can be gained about the nature of space-time inside this radius.

So what are we talking about when we talk about black holes, and how do we know whether what we say corresponds to what is out there? Hawking (Hawking and Penrose, 1997:3) cheerfully dismisses the question: *I take the positivist viewpoint that a physical theory is just a mathematical model and that it is meaningless to ask whether it corresponds to reality.* This is the view we came across earlier from James Jeans and it is disconcerting for the learner. Whether or not it is meaningless to look for correspondences between a theory and the world around us, that correspondence is what interests us at the rather fundamental level of wanting to learn what is what. If the elegant theories leading to the prediction of black holes are taken to be no more than tools for further predictions of the same kind, we are left wondering what this is all about. There is a peculiar symmetry here between the questions raised by physics and by mysticism: what, in the last resort, are we learning about through the procedures these disciplines commend? The mystic encounters God, the astrophysicist a black hole, but in neither case can we be sure, still less, say, what it is that has been encountered or indeed, whether what has been encountered is really there, ready to be disclosed to us as we follow the appropriate discipleship. What evidence is there in either case that will allow us to believe that we are talking about anything more than a closed system of self-referential axioms? We need the disciplines of mysticism and astrophysics to reassure us that their hold on reality has some sort of grip on reality. This they are unable to give since both are as in *The Waste Land* (Eliot, 1973): *Looking into the heart of light, the silence* – the heart of light which is paradoxically also the dark, the black hole, the cloud of unknowing: strangeness, otherness.

Learning, for both the astrophysicist and the mystic has to do with an object that cannot be directly experienced or known: neither the God of the mystic nor the black hole of the astrophysicist is knowable in any ordinary sense of the word. What sustains the mystic and the astrophysicist is a fascination, something akin to what Otto (1950) referred to as the *mysterium tremendum et fascinans*. There is something different out there. It is unknowable; we want to know it and we can't. It is other from us, strange, mysterious, the religious word is 'holy'. It is frightening because of its otherness and also because of its power: this is no small thing, but unimaginably powerful, hence the notion of its being *tremendous* – to be feared, to be wondered at. At the same time it is fascinating: we are drawn to it with desire and longing; in the case of the mystic with a yearning to be drawn into a relationship of ecstatic worship and of the astrophysicist to encounter something awesome about the way the universe works.

Rolle (1992:232) remarks *[The] mystery is hidden to many. A few, very special ones are shown it... it is given to those who must go through trials in this world of exile...* These quotations make uncomfortable reading: we are confronted by the unwelcome thought that this is an education for the élite: not everybody will benefit from it. The author of the *Cloud* is emphatic about this (1964:3):

> I charge thee and I beseech thee, with as much power and virtue as the bond of charity is sufficient to suffer, whatsoever thou be that this book shalt have in possession, whether by property, or by keeping, or by bearing as a messenger, or else by borrowing, that inasmuch as in thee by will and advisement, thou neither read it, write it, nor speak it, nor yet suffer it to be read, written, or spoken, by any other or to any other, unless it be by such a one or to such a one as hath (in thy supposing) in a true will and by a whole intent purposed him to be a perfect follower of Christ.

This is off-putting! Indeed, we seem to have encountered in this enquiry much that is fundamentally uncongenial to contemporary educational philosophy. Astrophysics and mysticism appear to have in common the rejection as an irrelevant distraction of student-centred learning, the repudiation of experience as misleading, and the claim, implicit in astrophysics, explicit in mysticism, that this is learning for the few: an élite, the chosen ones, distinct from the rest by their will to learn something unfathomable.

It is time to clarify the argument of this chapter. Both mysticism and astrophysics are élitist; unashamedly so. I said that Hawking was wrong to promise that all of us can be brought to understand the strangeness of the physics of the black hole: time standing still, matter compressed beyond anything that can be imagined. He is wrong but the impulse is loving: loving to the general public, who long to understand what he understands and loving towards his subject which is to him a matter of such fascination, and of such profound importance, that he passionately wants us to be brought to the recognition that he himself finds so astounding. It is an élitism of longing. What singles out the person who will come to this recognition is simply desire. We are going to need to want this encounter with something akin to the yearning of the mystic, if we are going to be sustained in the long and arduous discipleship which lies before us. We are going to need something like fanaticism in our motivation, otherwise we will not get there. As with astrophysics, so with mysticism: we have heard the *Cloud* insist that the contemplative is distinguished from the rest of us purely in terms of desire. This point is confirmed everywhere in the mystical writing of the time (Hilton, 1957:163; Julian of Norwich, 1998:84; Rolle, 1992:140).

What have we learned from putting our heads in the clouds? The simplest answer is to turn that question around, and to ask why students get bored. One reason suggested by Hayes (2003) is that nothing much in the way of learning is expected of them because there is nothing to be sure of, nothing securely to be known, and because of the privileging of skills over knowledge in the policies of contemporary educational managers and the politicians who direct them. Students are discouraged from believing that there is anything worth struggling to learn, particularly in the Arts and Humanities, and as a result of contemporary education policy, they would be prevented from studying it even if there were. We need to resist this view. This chapter has looked at two learning programmes which end in darkness; in each case the learner finds that darkness compelling, absolutely worth the effort of learning and training that has led to that encounter. If our curricula do not justify the effort, no-one will make the effort. Worse still, if our curricula are undemanding, students will conclude that there is little to learn, that they know it all, somehow or other, already. If the learning objective of our curricula is self-knowledge, students will indulge themselves in a frivolous way, secure in the conviction that they truly have nothing much to learn and that whatever they do learn will be of interest only to themselves, and then only passingly. There is something dreary about the view that I am the most interesting thing for me to learn about. There must be more interesting things than me for me to study. To suppose the opposite is a refusal to grow up. The argument of this chapter has been that the further you get from yourself as the object of the learning experience, the more compelling the learning becomes: strangeness and fascination go together. Lastly, we have seen that whilst it may be true that there is nothing certain in the way of knowledge, there is claimed to be something certain beyond knowledge. We do not know this tremendous strangeness; it is there; and it is worth learning to encounter.

(Note: I am deeply indebted to my colleague Phil Cragg, who spelled out the steps of the argument relating to astrophysics with great patience and lucidity.)

References

Anon (ed McCann, J) (1964) *The Cloud of Unknowing*. London: Burns and Oates

Cragg, P (2003) Black Holes, Big Bangs. Unpublished paper

Eliot, T (1973) *Selected Poems*. London: Faber

Forster, E M (2000) *Howard's End*. London. Penguin

Hawking, S (1995) *A Brief History of Time*. London: Bantam

Hawking, S and Penrose, R (1997) *The Nature of Space and Time*. Chichester: Princeton University Press

Hayes, D (2003) New Labour, New Professionalism, in: Satterthwaite, J, Atkinson, E and Gale, K (eds) (2003) *Discourse, Power, Resistance: Challenging the Rhetoric of Contemporary Education*. Stoke-on-Trent: Trentham Books

Hilton, W (Tr Sherley-Price, L) (1957) *The Ladder of Perfection*. Harmondsworth: Penguin

Jeans, J (1981) *Physics and Philosophy*. New York: Dover

Julian of Norwich (Tr Spearing, E) (1998) *Revelations of Divine Love*. Harmondsworth: Penguin

Keats, J (1973) Lamia, ll.234-237, in: *The Complete Poems*. London. Penguin

Otto, R (Tr Bracey, B) (1932) *Mysticism East and West: A Comparative Analysis of the Nature of Mysticism*. New York: Macmillan

Otto, R (Tr Harvey, J) (1923, 2nd ed. 1950) *The Idea of the Holy*. Oxford: Oxford University Press

Otto, R (Tr Lunn, B) (1931) *Religious Essays: A Supplement to The Idea of the Holy*. London: Oxford University Press

Phillips, A (2001) *The Physics of Stars (second edition)*. Chichester. John Wiley and Sons

Rolle, R (ed Backhouse, H) (1992) *The Fire of Love*. Sevenoaks: Hodder and Stoughton

Shelley, P (1977) One Word is too often profaned, in: *Selected Poems*. London: Dent

Stevenson, R L (1881) *Viginibus Puerisque and other Papers*. London: Kegan Paul

10

Doctors as connoisseurs of informational images: aesthetic and ethical self-forming through medical practice

ALAN BLEAKLEY

Alan Bleakley looks at a doctor looking at symptoms – or at what may, through the doctor's connoisseurship, constitute themselves in her/his imagination as symptomatic. Here is a way of knowing through aesthetic judgement – judgement, that is to say, informed by considerations of beauty, symmetry, elegance. For Bleakley, diagnosis is an art; but art is informational, and aesthetic judgement is sense-making. This chapter is poised between the cool wonderment of Satterthwaite and the discomforting disruptions of Danvers and Perselli, inviting us to reconstruct knowing as an ethical project.

Introduction

This chapter offers a test case for the main proposition of Michel Foucault's late work – that ethics can be conceived in terms of an art of self-fashioning as a purposive style of life, an ethos. Foucault confirms Nietzsche's announcement of the death of transcendental morality, to be replaced by *ethical* judgement relative to context and the particular needs of persons. However, a person must first shape the self into a form capable of tolerating the ambiguity inherent in exercising such a plural ethics. This shaping may be described as subscription to an open ended art of life, as an aesthetic commitment.

Stephen Greenblatt (1980) describes 'self fashioning' or 'self forming', a phenomenon first appearing during the Renaissance, as purposefully adopting an ethical stance as a response to some perceived authority or position with which one strongly disagrees. Taking up an ethical position in this way forms character or identity. Foucault (1987a, 1988, 1990), in a close reading of texts on style of life, traces such self-forming to Greek and Roman times, suggesting that this tradition disappeared in the Middle Ages, but reappeared with Modernism. For Foucault, however, the other against whom one pitches oneself in order to develop a style of life is oneself. It is the self that has become habitual, lazy and conventional and should be challenged in a permanent revolution of self against self. Thinking against oneself and thinking otherwise, in order to remake one's identity, is a critical feature of Modernism, now commonly referred to as reflexivity. This paper extends the ideas of both Greenblatt and Foucault in two ways, as an educational proposition. First, the art of existence as an ethical task is shifted into the sphere of work, as a central feature of vocation or calling. Second, the importance of thinking otherwise is extended to critique of habitual work practices and conventions as a vital aspect of occupational self-forming. The second idea develops Foucault's notion that normative discourses automatically produce the conditions of possibility for the emergence of resistances that can construct transgressive identities, where the latter may be a mark of innovation and reinvigoration. The focus of this chapter is the work, or vocation, of certain medical practitioners who typically grapple with visual clinical material within a specialty – tissue samples and gross specimens (histopathologist), skin (dermatologist) and mediated body images (radiologist).

Diagnosis from visible signs and symptoms is a culturally embedded practice. *Leviticus 13* in the Old Testament, written around 400 BC, describes 'how leprosy is to be recognised'. Amongst several diagnostic descriptions is the following: 'If the priest, looking at the place on (the) skin, finds that the hairs have turned white and the skin of the part affected seems shrunken compared with the rest of the skin around it, this is the scourge of leprosy.' The education of the eye ('seeing') is then paramount, and this was informed through comparison of the symptom with a vocabulary of carefully observed natural referents ('saying'). Rabbis identified over thirty shades of white in diagnosing leprosy, using referents such as wool, quicklime, snow, and 'the skin of an egg'. 'Seeing' and 'saying' are inseparable in the synthetic judgement that is the act of rapid diagnosis. Such judgement is the mark of expertise.

The Levitican priests, however, did not have the benefit of extended powers of perception through diagnostic imaging. Neither did they have scientific knowledge concerning causation and treatment of disease. However, where contemporary consultants make judgements in sense domains – such as working with visual clinical material – at the point of initial diagnosis the informing scientific knowledge of causation is suspended and secondary. The simultaneous descriptive 'seeing' and 'saying' of sense-based expert judgement precedes both explanation and prescription. The contemporary consultant is then acting like the Levitican priest, making a personal judgement based on the educated eye that makes sense of visual symptoms as significant configuration. While such an educated eye is gained through experience, it is open to refinement, further education and reformulation. With the forming of the expert eye also comes habitual, tired practice and unexamined convention that may paradoxically restrict expertise. Judgements in the sensory domain consist of discrimination between qualities, and education of such judgements is about enhancing sensitivity and acuity. The exercise of such discrimination is the practice of aesthetics, which literally means 'sense impressions'. To depress such discrimination, or to reduce the impact of such impressions, is to anaesthetise, numb, or produce insensitivity.

In what sense is such expert practice related to the composite Foucauldian theme 'discourse, power, resistance'? The Levitican example shows that the process of making a clinical judgement is a social practice that is rule-bound and historically contingent. Such a practice also serves to construct identities, ways in which the doctors in question see and present themselves, are seen by others, make meaning of the legitimacy of their work roles, and are positioned socially. Where a set of practices is legitimated, this also legitimates a certain kind of identity. This normative state generates the conditions of possibility for the emergence of resistance, as a deliberate critique of habitual practices.

Ethical and aesthetic self forming – an alternative to 'self discovery'

The normative post-Enlightenment discourse of the self is grounded in humanistic and existential notions of autonomy. It is normal for modern subjects to seek freedom from oppressive conditions within such a discourse. This is framed as an act of liberation or emancipation. Foucault (Burchell *et al*, 1991) challenges this conventional description of developmental autonomy as a form of 'governmentality'. He describes liberation of the self and its associated technologies as paradoxically offering a régime of control. Where the self, shifted from its grounding in post-Enlightenment humanism, is neither discovered nor liberated, Foucault resists the normative description of the self as *constitutive*. Rather, following Nietzsche, he describes a constituted self that may be formed or shaped aesthetically (O'Leary, 2002). Such aesthetic self-forming is the ethical act that resists the normative technical discourse of humanistic self-discovery and emancipation, and existential authenticity. Students of Foucault, eager to discover contemporary illustrative examples of his thesis on aesthetic and ethical self-forming, may be disappointed to find that such a model is derived from a detailed study of obscure Greek and Roman texts on morality, manners and stylised existence. This chapter provides a focused, contemporary example.

Foucault (in Rabinow, 1984:42) describes entry into an ethical practice in aesthetic terms, as the development of an 'arts of existence' through which an individual transforms the self and seeks 'being', ontology or a particular manner of existence, conduct. Thus, 'Modern man (sic) is not the man who goes off to discover himself, his secrets and his hidden truth; he is the man who tries to invent himself.' This person is faced with 'the task of producing himself'. In transposing Foucault's observations about styles of life in the Classical world to contemporary examples of professional working life, we can retain his notion that the character of such a style of life is best described through its intensity. Where Foucault (*ibid*:49-50) offers an aesthetics and ethics of self-forming for the modern era, he directs the reader towards acts of resistance through reflexive inquiry: 'the critique of what we are is at one and the same time an historical analysis of the limits that are imposed on us and an experiment with the possibility of going beyond them.' Lois McNay (1994:145) refers to 'The idea of an ethics rooted in interrogation of the limits of identity' with reference to Foucault's persistent theme of practices of transgression. Here, the aesthetics of existence is at its most intense, as the practitioner thinks against self, reflexively questioning habitual or restrictive practices. As Foucault (1982:216) suggests, 'the task nowadays is not to discover who we are, but to refuse what we are.' By this, Foucault means to refuse what we are normatively *defined* as. In defining how certain kinds of 'looking' and 'saying' offer resistance to the normative, technical-rational practices of the doctors discussed here, this chapter describes an *avant-garde* of medicine.

Expert judgement is a discourse

Foucault (1987a) notes that 'the way in which the subject constitutes himself in an *active fashion*, by the practices of the self (is) not something that the individual invents by himself. They are patterns that he finds in his culture'. This divides Foucault from the Kantian view that the autonomous self, or agent, is somehow floating free from its historical and cultural constitution, or is transcendental. For Foucault, the self is discursively produced and legitimated by the very techniques that supposedly discover and/or liberate the self (Bleakley, 2000). To appreciate the discursive production (discourse), maintenance (power) and possible disruption (resistance) of occupational identities, it is important to grasp the post-Foucauldian notion that discourses intersect, intertwine, interpenetrate and are nested (Torfing, 1999). There is no single discursive movement, moment or line, but webs, overlapping plateaux, or embedded structures in process. The identity production of doctors depends, at least, upon three nested discourses. First is the wider historical legitimation of the idea of an expert practitioner in science, whose idiosyncratic judgement is validated and valued within a community of practice. Second is socialisation into the wider values and practices of the medical profession. Third is socialisation into a specific community of practice or specialty as an expert 'consultant'. The main concern of this chapter is with the third of these processes, offering a particular focus upon expertise in judgement addressing visual sign and symptom. Discussion of the first point above, the discourse of idiosyncratic expert judgement in science, will clarify the notion of 'nested' discourses, prior to moving to point three: how has the idiosyncratic, subjective judgement of the scientist as expert come to be established as legitimate practice in a culture valorising objectivity and experimental evidence?

An experienced nurse in a post-operative recovery area makes a clear decision about the amount of analgesic to give a patient coming out of anaesthesia and waking up to post-operative pain. When asked why she gave that particular pain killer in that dosage, she says: 'It's very difficult to quantify. Every patient is different. I asked her how bad her pain was and made a decision.' Her clinical judgement did not fall from the sky. It reflects a discourse of nursing practice that nestles within a wider discourse of judgement in science. From a Foucauldian perspective, we might ask: 'how does a particular way of making expert judgements come to gain legitimacy, while another is marginalised as illegitimate?'

Peter Galison (1998) argues that since the establishment of science as a discipline in the late eighteenth to early nineteenth centuries, there have been three distinct historical phases with differing dominant discourses of decision making. Further, differing forms of scientific reasoning are embedded, nestle in, or intersect with, dominant moral climates and their guiding virtues. Prior to the 1830s, a Romantic notion of nature prevailed that harked back to Plato's view of the world as an imperfect representation of a concealed hidden order. Central to this movement was Goethe, and the key idea was genius. Certain people with genius had the vision to uncover nature's hidden order, despite her outer imperfections. Representations of nature such as drawings of plants should then not be descriptive, but inscriptive. The flower should be drawn to reveal its full geometric harmony, which may be exaggerated in the representation, as a move to perfect outer nature to align with a hidden order established through revelation. Such a discourse is nested in the wider cultural discourse of moral improvement. The identity constitution of the scientist as genius is explicitly elitist.

After 1830, and up to the first quarter of the twentieth century, objectivity becomes the dominant discourse in science. Prior to photography, the artist's hand must seek to make a faithful representation of a phenomenon. There is no hidden order to be revealed. Representations must be policed to check that there is no manipulation of the image. The advent of photography offers the ideal technology to support such objective practices of description and judgement in science, and the conscious suspension of subjective judgement for literal objective description becomes the norm. The scientist is then constituted as detached, passive observer, or as a Stoic.

By the mid-twentieth century, a new discourse arises that, paradoxically, legitimates both objectivity and subjectivity in scientific judgement at the same time. There is increasing value attached to the notion of the educated expert, or specialist, who is able to make idiosyncratic decisions from experience. Pure objectivity in judgement, 'propositional knowing' becomes evidence-based practice, exercised through protocols. Concurrently, the notion of an expert's subjective reasoning also becomes legitimate, exercised as professional judgement and interpretation. Active and interventionist expert reading is encouraged and an intellectual curriculum informs the process of judgement: through exercise of procedural (personal) knowing, (professional expertise gained through experience) as a counter to propositional knowing. Such professional expertise is validated through longer term membership of a community of practice. The ideal becomes an approximation and judgement becomes a reading of text, where the expert eye is educated. The new practitioner is reflective, sensitive, ethical and aesthetic. Professional practice is not just the exercise of judgement, but of conduct surrounding that judgement. The moral imperative is negotiated meaning rather than absolute truth, where judgement is now professional opinion rather than objective fact. Interpretation and judgement are cast as artistry and close reading of texts.

This shift in discourse led Ludwig Wittgenstein (1958), long before the current wave of social constructionists, to refer to science as a judgement-governed, rule-defying activity that does not *reflect* reality, but *produces* reality. Wittgenstein pointed out that scientific judgements are not necessarily criteria-led, but are based on logical similarity relations or homologies. Wittgenstein had introduced the notion of family resemblance in the early 1930s to capture a judgement-based, non-mechanical conceptual grouping. This kind of thinking is basic to pattern recognition, or the perceptual reasoning that characterises the rapid clinical diagnoses of experts. Such synthetic reasoning is termed 'abduction' by the pragmatist Charles Peirce (1998), as judgement based in sense discrimination, rather than the more cognitive judgements of induction and deduction. This follows

Baumgarten's (Welsch, 1997) project, in the mid-eighteenth century, to map aesthetics as sensory cognition. This notion is progressed to include an ecological component by contemporary models of dynamicist cognitive psychology, in which perception is described less in terms of inner, computational models, and more in terms of 'the use of repeated consultations of the world' (Clark and Eliasmith, 2002). Such activity has been modelled as an 'animate vision' paradigm, in which sensitivity to environmental cues is more important to judgement than stored cognitive maps (Clark, 1997).

Galison (1998) shows that in astronomy, particle physics and medicine, where visual judgements are central, experts learn an empirical art. Patterns are identified at a glance. Appeal is to the 'physiognomic gestalt' learned through experience, as socialisation into an agreed method for judgement within a community of practice such as medical specialties. Algorithms are avoided as restrictive because there is an inherent measure of uncertainty about normal variations within a group: 'Such a spectrum of the normal required exquisite judgement and extensive clinical training' (*ibid*:343). By using the word 'exquisite', Galison frames such judgements as aesthetic. This 'new form of scientific vizualisation' (*ibid*:349) constructs a particular identity or 'kind of persona' as 'interpreters' (*ibid*:351). Through the three historical periods, the 'scientist' then carries the virtue(s) inherent in the dominant discourse: 'genius' in the Romantic period, 'stoic' in early Modernism and 'interpreter' in late Modernism.

Drawing on Galison's model of differing historical constructions of the scientist helps to critically progress Foucault's examination of practices offering identity construction in terms of self-forming. Foucault expands the idea of aesthetic self-forming to a style of life or an 'aesthetics of existence': 'From the idea that the self is not given to us, I think that there is only one practical consequence: we have to create ourselves as a work of art.' (Rabinow, 1984). Foucault's model for such aesthetic self-forming as a style of life is Baudelaire's description of the dandy. The father of conceptual art, Marcel Duchamp, continues this tradition of self re-invention through a number of *alter egos*. The most famous of these was a woman, Rose Selavy (a pun on 'eros' and 'c'est la vie' – 'eros, that's life!').

Duchamp assumed the identity of Rose Selavy in 1920 and retired her in 1941. 'It was not to change my identity' that I invented Rose

Selavy, says Duchamp, 'but to have two identities' (Tomkins, 1997: 231). Lois McNay (1994:149), from a feminist perspective, criticises Foucault's valorisation of Baudelaire as privileging a male gendered exemplar of 'heroisation and mastery of the self'. An alternative to McNay's critique would be to suggest that Foucault's choice of hero shows an unexpected historical slippage. Duchamp or another modern transgressive thinker, who thinks otherwise and thinks against self, such as Wittgenstein, would perhaps have been a better example for Foucault to have chosen to illustrate his theme of self-forming. Both of these figures would fit Galison's description of the contemporary practitioner as interpreter, where Foucault's transgressive hero, Baudelaire, resurrects the Romantic tradition of artist as genius, now supplanted first by a discourse of scientific objectivity and second by a discourse of professional judgement as enshrining expertise. The self-forming of the contemporary medical expert is not best illustrated by returning to Baudelaire's Romantic dandy, but is better understood as modelling Galison's contemporary scientist-as-interpreter, where professional judgement is exercised through practice artistry.

The project: 'certainly, probably, maybe'

The author has set up an open ended collaboration between three consultant doctors and three experienced visual artists, entitled 'certainly, probably, maybe', reflecting the ever present sliding scale of uncertainty in clinical judgement (Bleakley *et al*, 2003a, 2003b). The inquiry is one of documentation of 'thinking aloud' through extended conversations. Artists visit clinics and laboratories and doctors visit studios. Participants anatomise clinical and aesthetic judgements and reflect after the event on the quality of judgement and alternative strategies. The artists provide a reconfiguration of the doctors' work that allows them to examine their practices from new angles, while the doctors provide artists with new material and ideas for their projects. Public forums such as seminars, conferences and publications encourage an innovative airing and re-framing of ideas. The project is embedded in a central medical educational question: how might aspects of clinical judgement be mapped and understood in order to enhance education? The focus in this chapter is on one aspect of this inquiry: how the aesthetic dimension of practice may shape identity of the doctors.

A key stimulus and inspiration for the project is the work of Felice Frankel (2002). Frankel is a photographer and artist in residence at the Massachusetts Institute of Technology (MIT). Over many years, she has helped scientists, particularly polymer chemists, to illustrate their work photographically for publication in prestigious journals such as *Science*. In the process of photographing, for example, a crystal structure or the surface of a polymer, Frankel provides a fresh look at the material. She does not enhance through computer manipulation, but uses lighting and framing or composition, such as innovative angles, that lead the scientists to look at materials with a reinvigorated eye, stimulating the imagination. She refreshes the senses of the scientists that may be habituated or saturated through constant exposure to particular stimuli.

The role of aesthetic environments – medicine as a cultural resource

Identity of medical practitioners as aesthetic practitioners is a product of the deliberate recognition of medicine as inherently aesthetic. Medicine is typically described as both an art and a science (Hunter, 1991). Donald Schön (1991) introduced the idea of deliberative or reflective practice in the professions as artistry to counter reduction to technical-rational description. As noted earlier, Galison has described the idiosyncratic artistry of the expert practitioner as the primary discursive construction of the contemporary scientist. While Schön alerts us to the value of thinking of professional identity as artistry, his failure to progress this notion to engage with practice style and aesthetic self-forming has been noted and critically progressed (Fish and Coles, 1998; Bleakley, 1999). Greenblatt's (1980) proposal is that self-forming or self-fashioning is a product of 'aesthetic structures that govern the generation of identities'. Contemporary medicine is replete with such aesthetic structures, where patients' signs and symptoms are already patterned and aesthetically arresting, and demand aesthetic response as discrimination through the senses or sensibility. Bodily symptoms are variously visually scanned, palpated, echo located or smelt.

Clinical judgement is often read as dehumanising or objectifying, evidenced in the 'seeing' of the clinical gaze (Foucault, 1973) and the 'saying' of the medicalised language of the case study and the diagnostic utterance (Hunter, 1991). However, this misses the point that such judgement can be humane while resisting grounding in a humanistic epistemology. Recall the distinction made earlier between self-discovery and self-forming. Self-forming can be a humane and ethically sensitive act without subscribing to a humanistic agenda of self-discovery. Indeed, one way of working on self as art is in the service of helping others. In contrast, humanistic self-discovery may be seen as self-centred. The work of defining professional practice in medicine as artistry can be focused upon the aesthetics of clinical judgement practices that collectively frame medicine as a cultural resource. Further, such judgement and its language may already be aesthetic and advertise medicine as a cultural resource. A radiologist faced with an x-ray of the sigmoid (the terminal part of the descending colon leading to the rectum), gives this description and diagnosis: 'This is a double contrast barium enema. There is an area of narrowing in the sigmoid. The under cut edges give an apple core appearance. This is colonic carcinoma.' The clipped language refers only to the object, to what is seen, and a clear diagnosis is reached.

There is a genre of Modernism – objectivism – that sets out to describe the object in its immediate appearance or self-presentation, just as the radiologist quoted above sets out to make a diagnosis through object reference. The American poet William Carlos Williams (who was also a family physician or general practitioner), at the height of his writing powers in the 1930s, describes his work as objectivist. Williams sets out to capture the object as given and reformulates the *haiku* style for a western audience:

The red wheelbarrow (1934)

so much depends
upon

a red wheel
barrow

glazed with rain
water

beside the white
chickens

Williams suggested that the poet 'must lift to the imagination those things which lie under the direct scrutiny of the senses, close to the nose.' Details must be illuminated or made 'phosphorescent'. If 'doctor' is substituted for 'poet', we have a clear description of abductive clinical judgement, as reasoning through the senses, with particular attention paid to the importance of detail as cue and clue. Williams says that there are 'no ideas but in things'. It is the visual, clinical material itself that educates the senses of the doctor through its self-display, where pattern recognition may be the expert's preliminary response in making a diagnosis. Such pattern recognition in expertise advertises a sensibility that on the outer is objectivist, even minimalist. The diagnostic utterance is stripped back, like a Modernist painting.

The Russian painter Kazimir Malevich, the originator of abstract painting, turned from figurative painting to a bold experiment in 1915. He painted first a crude red square on a white canvas. A black square painting followed and then a white square on white canvas, offering the first minimalist statement in painting. Malevich was also making a conceptual statement. He saw his reduction of form to basics as an outer expression of a complex reasoning and aesthetic process that remained tacit. Indeed, for Malevich, the outer process of stripping back offered a spiritual move akin to casting off material trappings or material binds, without losing touch with things. This resonates with Zen Buddhism's use of rich iconography as a tacit imaginational background, against which one exercises stripping-back to 'no-thing' without resorting to iconoclasm.

By 1913, Marcel Duchamp had already exhibited 'ready mades' or found objects, such as a hat stand and a urinal, in a gallery and art show, initiating conceptual art. This genre presents outwardly simple objects that carry complex subtexts. The art works by implication rather than explication. There is a striking parallel to be drawn between these visual art statements and their grounding in a certain kind of reasoning, Williams' objectivist poetry, and clinical judgement. Williams was surely moving back and forth between his clinical artistry and his poetry with some common purpose: he wrote observations for poems, and drafts, on prescription pads, both writing and clinical judgement forming an objectivist genre.

Studies of expert clinical reasoning suggest that stripped back, objectivist outer statements are informed by a complex cognitive process based on a storehouse of illness narratives, patient instances, heuristics (rules of thumb) and informing metaphors (Boshuizen, 1999). These constitute a clinical imagination that informs perception and allows for rapid diagnosis – often based upon pattern recognition (Bleakley *et al*, 2003a). This does not contradict the earlier observation concerning the value of a dynamicist cognitive psychology view of 'animate vision', where repeated consultations of the world tend to replace the need for elaborate inner representations. The perceptual process is enhanced, not replaced, by the clinical imagination, and this imagination is both ecological (worldly) and personal. Klemola and Norros (2001) suggest that better doctors embed personal judgement in a synthetic grasp of context or environment, with patient at the centre.

A further poem by William Carlos Williams perfectly illustrates the hiatus between outer, stripped back judgement within an objectivist genre, and the complex imagination that informs such clipped judgement:

Dish of Fruit (1944)

The table describes
nothing: four legs, by which
it becomes a table. Four lines,
by which it becomes a quatrain,

the poem that lifts the dish
of fruit, if we say it like
a table – how will it describe
the contents of the poem?

The poem describes the poet's reasoning or poetic imagination, and, by analogy, the clinical reasoning of the doctor. The poem's outer structure, a quatrain, is secondary to the poem's hidden treasures ('the contents') that is the 'dish of fruit'. Indeed, Williams cleverly constructs the poem so that the reader is forced to deconstruct the outer quatrain form to get the meaning. The poem described only in terms of the outer structure (quatrain) is like the 'table' described only in terms of 'four legs'. If we simply stick with the structure, how will we get at the rich content: the 'dish of fruit' that is lifted by the poem? The same is true of a clinical judgement: the outer, stripped back structure of medical language is a convention underneath which a 'dish of fruit' waits to be lifted. The dish of fruit is the rich, imagistic or metaphorical language and narrative examples that collectively constitute an expert's clinical imagination. Concurrently, that imagination is perceptually focused and worldly. It is an imagination of things or objects, not concepts. Indeed, as we learn from Duchamp and Malevich, the concept inhabits the object and its permutations of context.

Connoisseurship of informational images

Following Foucault's notion of self-forming as an alternative to humanistic self-discovery, we can reclaim what has been improperly stereotyped as medical dehumanising as a valid aesthetic position: objectivism. Through such reclamation of the aesthetic inherent to medical practices, we can also challenge the traditional, and un-helpful, separation of art and non-art, or informational, images. That medicine is inherently technical or instrumental, and not an aesthetic practice, is a view reinforced by the description of clinical images such as x-rays as 'scientific', 'non-expressive', 'utilitarian' or 'informa-tional' (Elkins, 1999). This traditional divide between informational and art images is, however, unsustainable, and counterproductive to practice framed as artistry. A pathology specimen or an x-ray may show intrinsic beauty. Indeed, many contemporary artists have turned to medical images and practices for their raw material. For example, the performance artist Orlan has turned aesthetic surgery into a feminist statement about standards of 'beauty'; and Mona Hatoum has turned an endoscopic exploration of her gut into a visually and aurally arresting projection, reminding the viewer that the 'inner' gut is an involuted surface.

Identity construction of the medical specialist through occupational self-forming can be described as 'connoisseurship', the term used res-pectively by Michael Polanyi (1998) to describe the exercise of tacit knowing, and Elliot Eisner (1979) to describe the educational imagination. This term is not used in an elitist or divisive sense, although it does refer to expertise and hence to specialist concerns. Connoisseurship is open to any expert in any field. Rather, it refers to the turning of technical expertise into an aesthetic sensitivity. Honouring the root meaning of the word, as 'one who knows', connoisseurship is what divides passive expertise, achieved through experience, from active expertise achieved through active reflection upon that experience. In the sensible world of the ordinary clinical work of the histopathologist, radiologist and dermatologist, an extraordinary imagination may be at work. The better clinicians are actively constructing style, as self-forming in aesthetically structured environments, not to know themselves better, the humanistic conceit, but to know their patients' symptoms for diagnostic accuracy better through education of sensibility. This work can be described as connoisseurship of informational images. Its adherents are likely to challenge instrumental conventions and functional bias within a medical specialty, and develop transgressive identities as forms of resistance to habitual, functional or un-aesthetic practices. These are special practitioners within specialties, defined by Klemola and Norros (2001) as 'interpretative' rather than 'reactive'. A parallel can be drawn between Galison's scientists-as-interpreters and medical practitioners engaged in aesthetic readings of symptom as text. Klemola and Norros (*ibid*: 455) describe such practitioners as creative, interactive, anticipative, sense-making and reflective, where 'professional behaviour' through 'interpretation and judgement' is summarised as 'artistry'.

References

Bleakley, A (1999) From Reflective Practice to Holistic Reflexivity, in: *Studies in Higher Education*, 24(3): 315-330

Bleakley, A (2000) Adrift Without a Life Belt: reflective self-assessment in a postmodern age, in: *Teaching in Higher Education*, 5(4): 405-418

Bleakley, A, Farrow, R, Gould, D and Marshall, R (2003a) Making sense of clinical reasoning: judgement and the evidence of the senses, in: *Medical Education*, 37(6): 544-552

Bleakley, A, Farrow, R, Gould, D and Marshall, R (2003b) Learning how to see: doctors making judgements in the visual domain, in: *Journal of Workplace Learning*, 15(7/8): 301-306

Boshuizen, H P A (1999) Medical Education; Or the Art of Keeping a Balance between Science and Pragmatics, in: McCormick, R and Paechter, C (eds) *Learning and Knowledge*. London: Paul Chapman Publishing

Burchell, G, Gordon, C and Miller, P (eds) (1991) *The Foucault Effect: Studies in Governmentality*. Hemel Hempstead: Harvester Wheatsheaf

Clark, A (1997) *Being there: Putting brain, body and world together again*. Cambridge, MA: MIT Press

Clark, A and Eliasmith, C (2002) Philosophical Issues in Brain Theory and Connectionism, in: Arbib, M A (ed) *The Handbook of Brain Theory and Neural Networks*. Cambridge, MA: MIT Press

Eisner, E (1979) *The Educational Imagination*. New York: Macmillan

Elkins, J (1999) *The Domain of Images*. London: Cornell University Press

Fish, D and Coles, C (1998) *Developing Professional Judgement in Health Care*. Oxford: Butterworth-Heinemann

Foucault, M (1973) *The Birth of the Clinic: An Archaeology of Medical Perception*. London: Tavistock

Foucault, M (1982) The Subject and Power, in: Dreyfus, H and Rabinow, P (eds) *Michel Foucault: Beyond structuralism and hermeneutics*. Chicago: University of Chicago Press

Foucault, M (1987a) The Ethic of Care for the Self as a Practice of Freedom, in: *Philosophy and Social Criticism*, 2: 112-131

Foucault, M (1987b) *The History of Sexuality Volume 1: An Introduction*. Harmondsworth: Penguin Books

Foucault, M (1988) *The History of Sexuality Volume 2: The Use of Pleasure*. Harmondsworth: Penguin Books

Foucault, M (1990) *The History of Sexuality Volume 3: The Care of the Self*. Harmondsworth: Penguin Books

Frankel, F (2002) *Envisioning Science: The Design and Craft of the Science Image*. London: MIT Press

Galison, P (1998) Judgement against Objectivity, in: Jones, C A and Galison, P (eds) *Picturing Science Producing Art*. London: Routledge

Greenblatt, S (1980) *Renaissance Self-Fashioning: From More to Shakespeare*. Chicago: The University of Chicago Press

Hunter, K M (1991) *Doctors' Stories: The Narrative Structure of Medical Knowledge*. Chichester: Princeton University Press

Klemola, U-M and Norros, L (2001) Practice-based criteria for assessing anaesthetists' habits of action: outline for a reflexive turn in practice, in: *Medical Education*, 35: 455-464

McNay, L (1994) *Foucault: A Critical Introduction*. Cambridge: Polity Press

O'Leary, T (2002) *Foucault: The Art of Ethics*. London: Continuum

Peirce, C S (1998) *The Essential Writings*. London: Prometheus Books

Polanyi, M (1998) *Personal Knowledge: Towards a Post-Critical Philosophy*. London: Routledge

Rabinow, P (ed) (1984) *The Foucault Reader*. New York: Pantheon Books

Schön, D (1991) *Educating the Reflective Practitioner: toward a new design for teaching and learning in the professions*. Oxford: Jossey-Bass Publishers

Tomkins, C (1997) *Duchamp: A Biography*. London: Chatto and Windus

Torfing, J (1999) *New Theories of Discourse: Laclau, Mouffe and Zizek*. Oxford: Blackwell

Welsch, W (1997) *Undoing Aesthetics*. London: Sage

Wittgenstein, L (1958) *Philosophical Investigations*. New York: MacMillan Co

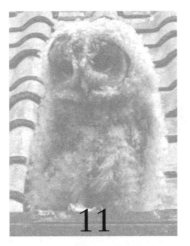

11

Stuttering at the owl:
poetic displacements and
emancipatory learning

JOHN DANVERS

In this challenging and unsettling chapter, John Danvers both promotes and practices resistance towards closure as a transformative pedagogic strategy. It is not an easy read; but it is not meant to be. It is in the very disruption of certainty, the poetic displacements and deliberate fragmentations that Danvers presents, that the potential for both making and questioning meaning lies. Why confront us with horses tethered in an art gallery, nomadic shelters, a glass igloo? Why tangle our minds with the fragmented phrases of Beckett, Wittgenstein and the Dadaist poets? Because by undoing the logic of language and the language of logic, Danvers argues, we can pay more attention to the architecture of signification that shapes our lives, and re-constitute ourselves as learners and teachers. Like Satterthwaite, Danvers obliges us to engage with the complexities of unknowing; like Bleakley, he invites us to use our aesthetic senses in the process; and like Perselli, whose chapter concludes this section, he expects us to construct our own multiple meanings from his text. In these ways, Danvers presents education as what Umberto Eco calls 'open work', and the process of disruptive meaning-making as a form of poetic resistance.

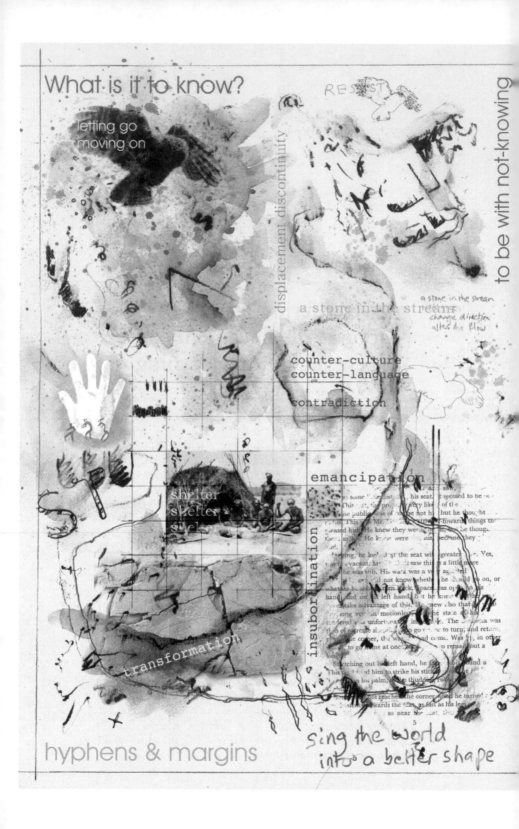

What is it to know?

letting go
moving on

displacement discontinuity

RESIST

to be with not-knowing

a stone in the stream
a stone in the stream
change direction
alter the flow

counter-culture
counter-language

contradiction

emancipation

shelter
shelter
shel

insubordination

transformation

hyphens & margins

sing the world
into a better shape

Introduction

I hope to show how the radical 'displacements and inventions' of certain kinds of poetic practices can and do act as an alternative to the dominant techno-rationalist discourses of many of our contemporary social and cultural institutions. Examples of non-linear writing, picturing and object-making will be presented as strategies of cultural resistance. I'll also briefly explore the implications of these practices and modes of being, knowing and doing, for the development of a more ludic pedagogy in which participation, indeterminacy and a transformative approach to learning are affirmed.

As an artist-learner-teacher working within a Buddhist-pragmatist framework, I am attempting to disinter and reconstruct an emancipatory project for learning and teaching through art practice. This could also be considered as aiming to develop and enact a radical pedagogy grounded in individual and collective transformation, critical scepticism and experiential engagement. (Danvers, 2003:47-57)

Atkinson (2002) has developed the idea of 'pedagogised identities' to describe the ways in which different learning and teaching contexts and normalising discourses, such as assessment régimes or developmental theories, produce different kinds of identity in learners and teachers. Within art education he argues that 'these discourses produce students' abilities in art practice' – a challenge to the view that these abilities are 'natural endowments' awaiting discovery or deployment. Recognising the power inherent in the vocabulary, syntax, register and mode of articulation used in a particular institutional discourse, also enables us to see the potential to disrupt or resist that power by modifying the syntax or destabilising the terms and structures of signification. To some extent we can reclaim control of our self-construction and cultural identity by developing a new counter-discourse and establishing affiliations with extant traditions of counter-discourse. Modern, postmodern, tribal and other radical poetries and arts practices provide examples of viable counter-discourses, both verbal, visual, material and spatial, which are explored in this chapter.

*

The text is organised in a series of discrete sections that illuminate different aspects of the field of enquiry. Each section is both free standing and in some way related to the others. The fragmentation and discontinuity within the text are presented as forms of resistance to normalising discourses of knowing, learning and being. The sequencing of text fragments is intended to surprise, to disrupt expectations and to encourage associative thinking on the part of the reader: an invitation to participate in the construction of meaning and interpretation.

Discontinuities and resistance

I open my book to an image of horses stabled in an art gallery. It is Rome, 1969. Jannis Kounellis is exhibiting the horses as art, or as a question mark in the face of art. The work is untitled. The horses move, make horse noises and fill the air with horse smells. Buckets and a broom stand in the corner.

Despite their location the horses resist categorisation as art. They pull at the ropes tethering them to the wall. The glare of gallery lights exposes every vein and mark on their skin.

We seek some resolution of our uncertainty. Why are they here? How are we expected to view them? What idea is the artist enacting? What does this spectacle mean?

There is nothing to help us. No explanation, title or commentary. All we have are eleven horses, being horses, tethered in a large, brightly lit, space.

*

In Samuel Beckett's novel, *Watt* (1970) the protagonist, Watt, watches and listens to the piano tuners, Mr Gall Senior and Junior:

> The mice have returned, he said.
> The elder said nothing. Watt wondered if he had heard.
> Nine dampers remain, said the younger, and an equal number of hammers.
> Not corresponding, I hope, said the elder.
> In one case, said the younger.
> The elder had nothing to say to this.
> The strings are in flitters, said the younger.
> The elder had nothing to say to this either.

The piano is doomed, in my opinion, said the younger.
The piano tuner also, said the elder.
The pianist also, said the younger.
This was perhaps the principal incident of Watt's early days in Mr.
Knott's house.

*

In October 1940, having left Paris for Vichy, Samuel Beckett joined
the French Resistance movement. In August and September 1942 he
was on the run from the Gestapo. According to Marjorie Perloff,
during these two months he was obliged to hide in many odd places,
including:

> ...the crawl space beneath the attic in Nathalie Sarraute's house
> (where Beckett was shut up for ten days in this suffocating space,
> together with Sarraute's aged and ill father); he spent a terrifying
> night in a tall tree in the woods... while below him the Germans
> made periodic patrols with dogs and guns; and later, he and
> Suzanne hid in a series of barns, sheds, and haystacks on the way
> to the south, walking only at night when they were relatively safe.
> When they finally arrived at the village of Rousillon... they were in
> a state of physical and mental exhaustion. (Perloff, 1996:125)

Perloff makes a very persuasive argument for linking Beckett's involvement in the Resistance, and particularly the use of a complex
'cut-out' system used by his 'Gloria' cell to prevent infiltration, and
the compositional structure of his novel *Watt*. The 'cut-out' system
ensured that discrete fragments of information were passed on from
person to person so that only the person at the end of the chain could
fit the fragments together and make sense of the whole. *Watt* was
written by Beckett in short bursts during the five-year period from
1940-45, coinciding almost exactly with his Resistance experiences.
The novel is full of discontinuities, non-sequiturs and uncertainties. In
Perloff's words: 'Plot counts for very little, one event never logically
leading to another and interruption (in the form of poems, songs, lists,
and charts) occurring frequently.' 'No character, no plot, no symbols,
where none intended' – as Beckett famously put it. (Perloff, 1996:
126)

Prior to the writing of *Watt*, in 1937 Beckett had noted:

It is indeed becoming more and more difficult, even senseless, for me to write an official English. And more and more my own language appears to me like a veil that must be torn apart in order to get at things (or the Nothingness) behind it... Let us hope the time will come, thank God that in certain circles it has already come, when language is most efficiently used where it is being most efficiently misused. (Perloff, 1996: 120)

Beckett strives to resist the formulaic structures of 'official English', to usurp the power of the dominant discourse by disrupting the sound surface of the language. (Perloff, 1996: 121) In relation to Beckett, Perloff argues, 'The resistance to language... must be understood in terms of 'the language of Resistance" (Perloff, 1996: 22).

*

In his song, *Til I Die,* Brian Wilson, the elderly Beach Boy, writes: 'I'm a leaf on a windy day/Pretty soon I'll be blown away.'

*

Wittgenstein, in his *Notes on Logic* (1914-16/1979) writes: 'Distrust of grammar... is the first principle of philosophising. And, by extension, of poeticising.' (Perloff, 1996: 17) In the *Philosophical Investigations* (1958) he resists imposing an artificial continuity on his own thinking and writing, even an organic linearity, because it would constrain his criss-crossing, disjunctive patterns of thought: what Perloff calls his 'revisionary' methods of composition. This process of sustained uncertainty and indeterminacy becomes a tacit benchmark of a new kind of philosophical practice, which involves both a critique and a revisioning of language through the use of anecdote, enigmatic utterance, associative imaging, seriousness and playfulness, assertion and counter-assertion. The need to destabilise, to jolt the reader out of his or her preconceptions and intellectual comforts becomes an important part of Wittgenstein's philosophical project.

This description of philosophical method could also be used as a manifesto for learning and teaching. Embracing the equivocal indeterminacy of language as a given, we can see learning and teaching as a discontinuous series of dialogue events, an exchange of conundrums, puzzles, uncertainties and ponderings that gradually liberate us from the tyranny of 'unthinking' (to use e.e.cummings' term), enabling us to resist in small ways the hegemonic structures of institutional discourses that demand a relatively supine acceptance. cummings employs all manner of grammatical and typographic devices and displacements as a form of resistance to the normalising power of the conventional sentence. He prods us out of unthinking into linguistic attentiveness and engagement:

> all ignorance toboggans into know
> and trudges up to ignorance again:
>
> ...
>
> one's not half. It's two are halves of one:
>
> ...
>
> pity this busy monster, manunkind
> (cummings, 1963: 65, 57, 56)

As Ingeborg Bachman puts it, there are times when one has to be

> ...against every metaphor, every sound, every rule for putting things together, against... the inspired arrival of words and images... suspicion is important... suspect the words, the language. (Bachmann, 1991, in Perloff, 1996: 151. Perloff's translation.)

This suspicion helps us to resist the institutional construction of the subject: the technocratic determinacy that builds subject identities through conformity to dominant patterns of language, behaviour, desire and sublimation. The identification and deconstruction of these dominant patterns is central to a view of learning as a transformative and emancipatory project, enabling each of us to re-constitute our subjectivity in new ways, to reformulate ourselves in terms other than those we are given by context, habit, or the 'official English' of rule-making institutions and traditions.

*

On the other hand, confounding expectations should not become a new orthodoxy. Vermeer can be as liberating as Damien Hirst.

Unlearning, unknowing and letting go

What is it to know? Are learning and knowing synonymous? Is to learn to know, or to be with not-knowing to be dynamically resigned to uncertainty and to an open ended series of speculations? Unlearning is an important process within art education, a disciplined letting go of habits of thought and practice. Unlearning, unknowing, letting go and wordlessness can be seen as modes of being and doing (or undoing) that contrast with, though dynamically related to, rational, acquisitive, worded and cognitive modes. Learning and unlearning involve destabilisation, transformation, change, processes of dissolving opacity, undoing knots, but only to move to the next knot, the next eddy in the flow. All we can do is exchange one conundrum for another in a process that is more akin to free association than logical progression or problem solving.

*

Tristan Tzara – from *The Approximate Man*

> I think of the heat that language weaves
> – around its core the dream they call us by
> (in Rothenburg and Joris, 1995: 499)

*

Beckett told Tom Driver in a 1961 interview:

> We cannot listen to a conversation for five minutes without being acutely aware of the confusion. It is all around us and our only chance now is to let it in. The only chance of renovation is to open our eyes and see the mess. It is not a mess you can make sense of. (in Perloff, 1996: 133)

Beckett may have in mind a process of renovating our selves, reconstituting the subject. If renovation is to happen in educational contexts, if we are to reconstitute ourselves, we need to open our eyes, see the mess and let in the confusion.

*

Questions like, 'What does it mean?' may be irrelevant and inapplicable to many art practices and products, and to many events and situations in the (dis)course of life. The rising sun does not mean anything, nor does the Mona Lisa. Facts and artefacts do not provide predetermined meanings; instead they are the non-signifying context within which we temporarily rest to build the shelters which are our selves. We make these shelters of words, signs and gestures from which to engage our surroundings for a moment before we break camp, throw water on the fire and move on to make another shelter, and another.

172

The materials for our shelter making are those that others also use. Protocols of usage can come to govern what we do and how we build, to the point that we begin to move into prefabricated structures and enact prefabricated lives. Somehow the exercise of poetic resistance and 'suspicion' enables us to make bespoke shelters of words, signs and gestures that are more like a tent or bivouac than a house, more like clothing or a second skin. The temporariness of selfhood is permanent, even if we imagine it to be otherwise.

*

Out in the desert, a man lived in a hut. To him it was nothing special. He'd lived in many places. This was just another in a long line. Maybe they weren't all as small as this, nor as temporary, but this was much like its predecessors. Four walls, a roof, a doorway (though no door). No windows. But light came in through the many holes and openings. A space, refuge, shelter. Somewhere out of the sun and the wind.

Some say the tin shack accounted for his cryptic speech, his non-sequitorial grammar, the 'salmon leaps' of his utterances. Others thought he'd brought these with him from a life of wandering, the disjointed travels echoed in his disjointed discourse. He moved from place to place, not in search of something, or running away from something, but somehow as a statement of being at home anywhere. He was always at home. Yet he was also both an immigrant and an *émigré* wherever he went.

*

Two lovely words: 'dromomania' – an abnormal, obsessive desire to roam; and 'drapetomania' – an uncontrollable desire to wander away from home.

*

Beckett's Cast-offs:

> once safely navigated life all over extinction ~ from the unuttered parenthesis the first cliché ~ yet art is a longer perspective ~ annihilation, dignified in its own way, is a stylistic change ~ he told me to disappear in vain ~ blown roses left in peace, humus mingled with the here dead set down shaft of dark in the Rue de Seine ~ back over the years, forty years of neglect intimate to us ~ and this was brevity, perhaps breathing or extinguishing, glimpsed for the

first time only as it is going darting besieged by inexistence ~ a lengthy episode in many filaments ~ tenderly the needle stops mid-stitch (Danvers, 1999)

*

In May 1917, the Dadaist poet and performer, Hugo Ball, writes in his diary:

> in these phonetic poems we totally renounce the language that journalism has abused and corrupted. We must return to the innermost alchemy of the word; we must even give up the word too, to keep for poetry its last and holiest refuge... (in Cobbing and Griffiths, 1992: 341)

Here's an example of one of Ball's phonetic poems, titled: *Sea Horses & Flying Fish*:

tressli bessli nebogen leila
flusch kata
ballubasch
zack hitti zopp

zack hitti zopp
hitti betzli betzli
prusch kata
ballubasch

fasch kitti bimm
zitti kitillabi billabi billabi
zikko di zakkobam
fisch kitti bisch

bumbalo bumbalo bumbalo bambo
zitti kitillabi
zack hitti zopp

(in Rothenberg and Joris, 1995: 297)

*

Jerome Rothenberg proposes his 'ethnopoetics' as a 'counter-language' to the deadening clichés of official institutionalised languages (Rothenberg, 1994). He gathers examples of such a poetics in a number of anthologies that bring together poetries and songs from the oral traditions of native tribal peoples around the world, alongside radical Modern and post Modern texts that disturb the smooth syntax and semantics of the dominant discourse (see Rothenberg, 1969; Rothenberg and Joris, 1995 and 1998). The anthology becomes a mode of cultural dialogue and a statement of cultural resistance to the beliefs, values and practices of technocratic and bureaucratic instrumentalism, providing alternative voices to the rhetoric of efficiency, accountability and other managerial orthodoxies. Rothenberg affirms the value of multiplicity and diversity, of polymorphous languages and identities: a plurality of being, knowing and doing, rather than the pursuit of enduring certainties and conformity, or of terms and phrases that offer solutions, or of vocabularies that aim to pin down, fix, define, judge or quantify.

Hybrids, hyphens and margins

These ideas can be linked to the work of the Chinese/Canadian poet, Fred Wah. In his poetry and poetics Wah explores the 'hyphened position, a hybridised identity'. He writes:

> The half-breed shares with the nomadic and diasporic, and the immigrant, the terms of displacement and marginalisation. Yet the hybrid, even in those relegated spaces of race and ethnicity, is never whole. It is the betweenness itself, however, that becomes interesting. (Wah, 2002)

This notion of the 'hyphened position' can also be applied to any of us trying to survive existentially, poetically and ethically within a comforting but alienating technocratic culture. Many of us are marginalised, forced into a cultural nomadism in which we seek out voices and positions that articulate alternatives, enabling us, temporarily at least, to feel kinship. Those voices and positions may belong to radical Modern or post Modern artists and poets, tribal songmakers, scattered mythmakers and mythcritics, or passing individuals who light up the street and transform everyday experience.

Wah continues:

> The discourses of other marginalised positions have always interested me as fodder for a resistance to being a fixture of colonisation. Writers have to make choices about language and when you're writing in the language of the coloniser any overt play against the grain can be generative. (Wah, 2002)

Many of us have to write in the language of the coloniser within our professional roles, and find ways of playing against the grain in order to regenerate and enliven ourselves.

Within learning and teaching we have to find ways to enable students to live and speak against the grain, to recognise their own hybridity and to establish kinship with others, however distant in time and space, who share a hyphened position at the margins of the dominant technocracy.

Education as 'open work' – a multitude of stories

How can we resist the encroachment of narrowly focused utilitarianism and determinism in the fields of learning and teaching? Working under the reductionist banners of 'preparation for work', 'employability', 'accountability', 'learning outcomes', 'learning contracts', etc, we lose sight of a more emancipatory and transformative view of education and of the need to develop our citizens as human beings, alive to themselves, to each other and to the world in which we live.

In order to become more fully alive, to be open to experience and to reconstitute ourselves day by day we need to find ways in which our gifts, skills and aspirations can be identified, developed and exercised within a conceptual framework that is questioning, critical and analytical as well as attentive, celebratory and able to sing. We need to be able to distinguish between important and unimportant needs and to separate out the strands of manipulation and coercion that all social institutions deploy. We need to embrace the discontinuities of life and the endless puzzles that engage us as learners, in order to teach in ways that are indeterminate and open, allowing those we teach to interpret, make meaning and demonstrate learning in surprising stories and inventive actions and forms.

Philosophical thinking, as exemplified by Wittgenstein's distrust of grammar, Bachmann's suspicion of the words, and Beckett's tearing apart of official English, has to be worked for at all ages and in all the contexts of learning, formal and informal. This kind of thinking can be related to Foucault's archaeological methods of discourse analysis (1972, 1977), Derrida's deconstruction of the binary structures of inclusion and exclusion (1976) and the pragmatist critiques of social and intellectual institutions articulated by Richard Rorty (1999).

Rorty argues that the socialising function of education needs to be counter-balanced, or even subverted, by an'individualising' function that involves '... a matter of inciting doubt and stimulating imagination' in order to foster 'self-creation' (1999: 118). The ability to sniff out the convoluted, multi-layered, mycelia of power has to be matched by the capability of constructing alternative structures of signification: to disturb and revitalise familiar patterns of discourse with new songs, stories, actions and images.

*

Robert Smithson, in his 1966 essay, *Sedimentation of the Mind*, writes:

> Words and rocks contain a language that follows a syntax of splits and ruptures. ...This discomforting language of fragmentation offers no easy *gestalt* solution; the certainties of didactic discourse are hurled into the erosion of the poetic principle. (Flam, 1996)

*

An open igloo made of metal struts and sheets of glass stands in a gallery space, with a bare limbed branch protruding from the top. The artist, Mario Merz, calls it: *Igloo with a Tree*. The story-maker inside us begins to stir. We see it as a statement about the colonisation of tribal peoples, or the expropriation of vernacular architecture by late Modernist European high art, or a witty juxtaposition of tree and arctic houseform. The ancient symbol of a tree of life points to some kind of resurrection of ethnicity in the face of global capitalism.

The structural simplicity of the shelter points to a post-industrial age of subsistence architecture in which we endlessly recycle materials. We shudder at the way the branch seems to be trying to escape the glass-toothed dome, a leafless dying gesture of resistance, memorial to a way of life no longer sustainable. We notice the glass reflects back at us our own image as coloniser, a consumer eager to find a new taste to stimulate our easily jaded palettes. And yet we can also see through the glass, through the domed form, taking in the rest of the room, seeing other spectators eating the art in the same hurried manner.

We voice all these stories and more. And none seems more true than another. There is no mono-meaning, no single content or point, only multiple stories woven around the spare arcs of metal, planes of glass and filigree of wood. There is also wordless wonder, perplexity or surprise, a mute engagement or silent encounter with the art work. In the end it defies consumption, it is both meaningless and meaning-full, valueless and invaluable.

Umberto Eco (1989) provides us with some kind of academic legitimation for our varied interpretations: an open igloo a perfect exemplar of his 'open work'. According to Eco the 'open work' constitutes 'a field of open possibilities' (p86) arising from 'its susceptibility to countless different interpretations which do not impinge on its unadulterable specificity. Hence, every reception of a work of art is both an interpretation and a performance of it' (p4). Eco refers to Pousseur, who 'observed that the poetics of the 'open' work tends to encourage 'acts of conscious freedom' on the part of the performer and place him at the focal point of a network of limitless interrelationships...'. (Eco, 1989: 4)

Education, the processes of learning and teaching, can be seen as an 'open work' leading to unpredictable stories, meanings and changes of mind. In this view of education, learner and teacher are active participants in personal and collective acts of story-making, and learning is always indeterminate as to outcomes. Rather than consumers of education we are producers of learning, enacting or performing our learning within 'a field of open possibilities'.

*

Tristan Tzara – from *The Approximate Man*:

> what is this language whipping us we jump at lights
> our nerves are whips held in the hands of time
> and doubt comes with a single faded wing
> screws into us and squeezes presses deep inside
> like wrappers crumpled in an empty box
> gifts of another age to swirls of bitter fish
> (in Rothenberg and Joris, 1995: 496)

The insubordination of words

Guy Debord (in Rothenberg and Joris, 1998: 419) reminds us that though words and images are 'employed *almost constantly*, exploited full time for every sense and nonsense that can be squeezed out of them, they still remain in some sense fundamentally strange and foreign... We should also understand the phenomenon of the *insubordination* of words [and images], their desertion, their open resistance,' which is manifested in many forms of poetries, artefacts and performances. These forms displace the *status quo* and the given, in favour of the unexpected and subversive. I once heard the poet, Gary Snyder, in a radio interview, refer to this subversive quality in poetry as the 'stuttering voice of revelation'.

*

This brings to mind Coleridge's notebooks, fragmentary records of his myriad-mindedness, manifestations of the 'flux and reflux of the mind in all its subtlest thoughts and feelings' (Perry, 2002: vii). According to Perry, 'it was the Notebook, in its unplanned, unfolding, various existence, which allowed his multiform genius its natural outlet' (*ibid*: viii). Coleridge resisted the temptation, or pressure, to unify and synthesise his material, instead he aimed to be true to 'his mind's immense and multiple activity, in all its unmeeting extremes' (*ibid*).

*

Debord (Rothenberg and Joris, 1998: 419) points to the opposition between 'informationism', the discourses of bureaucracy, officialdom and consumerism, and radical, transformational poetries, philosophies and arts, those kinds of poetry, philosophy and art that make us sit up and take notice, pay attention to the architecture of signification, and become open to changes of mind, revisions of self and subjecthood.

These fault lines can be extended into the terrain of education, where informationism and managerial determinacy can be counteracted by emancipatory teaching strategies that foreground learning as a process of expanding critical and imaginative powers, an open work in which we each develop a voice to sing the world into a better shape, or make objects and performances that revision life's potential and actuality.

In economic, social and cultural spheres we face a kind of creeping totalitarianism that is already close to sweeping away dissent and diversity. Cultures of teaching and learning are reinforced by, and reinforce in their turn, the narrow minded controlling impulse of government and big business, a powerful managerialism that values conformity to process and method above the development of aspiration, imagination, understanding and engagement. Passivity, resignation and a feeling that change is impossible are both symptomatic of alienation and disillusionment and a necessary condition of particular kinds of political and economic structures. In the dialogues and encounters that lie at the heart of learning and teaching, we can expose these structures, reclaim and revitalise alternative traditions and open up new ways of thinking, articulating and acting.

*

A Verdi Chimney For Jannis (Danvers, 1999)

(text constructed from fragments of a Jannis Kounellis exhibition catalogue, Van Abbemuseum, Holland 1981)

As Rimbaud said in a letter to Paul Demeny, 15 May 1871: 'every poet is a thief of fire'

... all his life he wanted to paint among the ruins but time was against him ~ in a sense it is like being ~ mostly the weather is clear, then grey ~ it is like being a refugee, a little cloud ~ stabled horses are a sign ~ nomads are not tramps ~ it is like being on a ship, burning laurel at the beginning of time, broken sculpture in the sun, St John the Baptist, a white horse, a blackbird ~ old silence like a rose, a train, a border guard

everyone has a right to think, to be nervous, to abandon history ~ every word is a small oil lamp and provides just enough light

*

In *S/Z*, Roland Barthes writes about the 'writerly text' as being indeterminate in meaning, open to a plurality of readings, based as it is on the 'infinity of languages' (1990: 5). Applying the practices of radical poets, artists, mythmakers and mythcritics can become a vital part of an emancipatory approach to learning and teaching, a project in which we as teachers and learners become active producers rather than passive consumers.

Coda

In his book *The Spell of the Sensuous,* Abrams (1997:87-88) describes how the Cree peoples of North America believe that owls can cause stuttering and an incapacity to speak. Yet if they hear stuttering they are fascinated by it. If you go into the woods and stutter, an owl is likely to turn up. At which point you can interrogate it, argue with it, and perhaps liberate it from its own mental and behavioural habits.

Maybe, by stuttering a new poetic syntax, we can resist and overturn the process by which the owls of officialdom render us incapable of vital speech, establishing for ourselves a renewed, hyphened identity through the subversive deployment of stories, objects, gestures and actions that are both critical and transformative. By stuttering at the owls of officialdom we might be liberated from the stifling mental and behavioural habits they impose on us and maybe officialdom will itself be transformed, becoming more open to many voices and stories.

Owls: Photo-images by John Danvers

References

Abrams, D (1997) *The Spell of the Sensuous*. New York: Vintage Books

Atkinson, D (2002) *Art in Education: Identity and Practice*. The Netherlands: Kluwer Academic Publishers

Bachmann, I (1991) *Wir Müssen Wahre Sätze Finden: Gesprache und Interviews*. Munich: R Pier and Co

Barthes, R (1990) *S/Z*. Oxford: Blackwell

Beckett, S (1970) *Watt*. New York: Grove Press. (Originally published in 1953 by John Calder, London)

cobbing, b and griffiths, b (eds) (1992) *Verbi Visi Voco: A Performance of Poetry*. London: Writers Forum

cummings, e e (1963) *selected poems: 1923-1958*. London: Penguin

Danvers, J (1999) *Remnants*. Artist's book, privately published: limited edition. (No page numbers)

Danvers, J (2003) Towards a radical pedagogy: provisional notes on learning and teaching in art and design, in: *International Journal of Art and Design Education*, 22(1): 47-57

Derrida, J (1976) *Of Grammatology*. Baltimore and London: Johns Hopkins University Press

Eco, U (1989) *The Open Work*. Cambridge, MA: Harvard University Press

Flam, J (ed) (1996) *Robert Smithson: The Collected Writings*. Berkeley and Los Angeles: University of California Press

Foucault, M (1972) *The Archaeology of Knowledge*. New York: Pantheon

Foucault, M (1977) *Discipline and Punish: The birth of the prison*. New York: Pantheon

Perloff, M (1996) *Wittgenstein's Ladder: Poetic language and the strangeness of the ordinary*. Chicago: University of Chicago Press

Perry, S (ed) (2002) *Coleridge's Notebooks: A selection*. Oxford: Oxford University Press

Rorty, R (1999) *Philosophy and Social Hope*. London: Penguin Books

Rothenberg, J (ed) (1969) *Technicians of the Sacred: A range of poetries from Africa, America, Asia and Oceania*. New York: Anchor Books

Rothenberg, J (1994) Ethnopoetics at the Millenium. A Talk for the Modern Language Association, December 29, 1994. http://wings.buffalo.edu/epc/authors/rothenberg/ethnopoetics.html accessed 02/10/2002

Rothenberg, J and Joris, P (1995) *Poems for the Millennium, Volume One*. Berkeley and Los Angeles: University of California Press

Rothenberg, J and Joris, P (1998) *Poems for the Millennium, Volume Two*. Berkeley and Los Angeles: University of California Press

Smithson, R (1966) Sedimentation of the mind, in: Holt, N (ed) (1979) *The Writings of Robert Smithson*. New York: New York University Press

Wah, F (2002) Interview with Fred Wah. http://www3.sympatico.ca/pdarbyshire/wah.html accessed 14/10/2002 (No page numbers)

Wittgenstein, L (1958) *Philosophical Investigations*. New York: Macmillan

Wittgenstein, L (1979) Notes on Logic, in: Wittgenstein, L *Notebooks 1914-1916*. Chicago and London: University of Chicago Press

12

'A personal preview': or 'Portraying my professional life in pictures'
Image and performance as methodology for research in teaching and learning

VICTORIA PERSELLI

In this concluding chapter, Victoria Perselli follows John Danvers' theme of poetic resistance, using visual art, narrative, metaphor and performance. Perselli invites us to take a series of intellectual side-steps in order to distance ourselves from the daily experience of being a teacher, achieving this effect of distantiation by inviting us to view her professional life – and her research – as a series of pictures, with herself as the artist. However, this is no quick-flip album of easy snapshots: these images (which she presents as metaphors), are heavily imbued with social, cultural, personal and political resonances, some of which we may connect with, while others may pass us by completely. This is just what the author/artist expects: while she demands (or hopes) that we will work hard at making connections and reading her text as we might 'read' montage, patchwork or jazz music, she also requests that we accept the partial nature of our understanding, both as an example of and as a metaphor for the intangible, slippery nature of what actually goes on in the layering of experience that makes a teacher or learner. The final section of the chapter is written, and therefore needs to be read, as a performance piece, in which the reader is invited to follow the rhythm and flow of the language, without necessarily striving constantly after meaning: as Perselli put it in discussion with the editor, 'meaning' here has connotations beyond the linguistic turn. Here, a host of themes and characters come together to shape a life: authors and poets; musicians and composers; educationists and philosophers; pupils, teachers and parents. Through metaphorical and allegorical play with notions of authorship and ownership, power and resistance, gender and identity, Perselli challenges us to re-examine our practices and to reassert the immense significance of actual people and places, as well as of memory, imagination and desire, in the formation of selfhood in teaching and learning.

For madness isn't such a terrible thing
madness isn't half-blind.
Madness can talk, can laugh and dance
madness can sing.
And I am more than just the sum
of all my grief.
And in that –
I am *accountable* to no-one.
V.P. Research Diary, Sept. 1995

Introduction

Researchers in education have become increasingly interested in diverse interpretive media and forms of representation (Weber and Mitchell, 1995; Prosser, 1998; Cole and McIntyre, 1998; Winter, Buck and Sobiechowska, 1999; Gazetas, 2000; Schratz, 2001; Walker, 2001; Perselli, 2004a, 2004b, 2004c), through narrative fiction, autobiography, film, video, photography and dance. This is congruent with postmodern conceptualisations of culture and of arts media as a means towards hearing and seeing multiple voices and perspectives on a given phenomenon, or simply towards understanding in new ways the multidimensional nature of human interactions and experiences, of which education forms a significant part.

In *Border Crossings*, for example, Henry Giroux (1992: 21) calls for

[a] politics and pedagogy developed around new languages capable of acknowledging the multiple, contradictory and complex subject positionings people occupy within different social, cultural and economic locations.

184

He identifies a need

> to take up the relationship between language and the issues of knowledge and power on the one hand and to retheorise language within a broader politics of democracy, culture and pedagogy on the other. This suggests creating a new language that extends the meaning of pedagogy as a form of cultural production that takes place in a variety of sites and is produced by a diverse number of cultural workers. (*Ibid*)

He is unequivocal in stating that postmodernist theorising, especially when combined with modernist and feminist perspectives, can offer hope for the future as well as providing a radical critique of the present, when he speaks of

> a politics and a set of pedagogical practices that can refigure and change existing narratives of domination into images and concrete instances of a future that is worth fighting for. (Giroux, 1992: 78)

Taking a broad interpretive sweep on Giroux's advocacy of 'a new language', I will endeavour to demonstrate some of the methodological means by which I have used arts media, in particular visual imagery and dramatic representation, to come to a radical reconceptualisation of my practice as a coordinator for special educational needs (SENCO) in mainstream infant education (ages four to seven), in the south east of England.

Researching the role of SENCO

The Linguistic Turn

One of my intentions in this study (Hamilton *et al,* 1998; Bullough and Pinnegar, 2001: 13-23) of my practice, researched over the period 1995-2000, was to try to collapse the boundaries of SEN/Inclusion. Over time these apparent umbrella terms had come to signify a discrete and increasingly regimented set of activities: the assessment, testing, categorisation and labelling of individual learners; the formulation of Individual Education Plans and Targets; the differentiated teaching provision, largely focused on English and mathematics, towards predetermined national attainment levels; the ubiquitous rounds of audits and bids for funding of SEN provision. All of this left no space for truly innovative teaching or curriculum development, which ran the risk of punishment for non-compliance with both recent legislation and the standards set and enforced by the national inspection régime for England and Wales. My initial concern in the research was the extent to which these activities had come to define and shape the identities of teachers and learners, so that the overarching theme of the study emerged as a story of resistance: firstly to technical rationalism, medicalisation and the deficit model of SEN as characterised by the procedures and underlying ideology of the SENCO role (for closely comparable issues related to mentoring, see Colley, 2003) and secondly towards my increasing feelings of disaffection and alienation from teaching.

The work of postmodern writers such as Giroux gained importance at the point in the study where I began to recognise the many influences in and around my working life not governed by the dominant discourses of instrumentalism or medicalisation, that pertained rather to the complex cultural, economic and social locations in which I, and my infant pupils, were situated. Whilst I had not initially intended any part of the research to be presented as Art or Performance, I found that the most effective way of conveying its complexity: who I saw myself to be, how I worked with children, where my personal cultural influences and past experiences seemed to inform my present-day SENCO persona was via a series of poems, stories and eventually dramatic duologues, all of which lent themselves to live performance.

By engaging the notion of imaginative conjecture when thinking about the SENCO role in relation to teaching and learning, I found myself freed up to pose a different set of identity-related questions: If I were a story teller, how would I narrate this? If I were a visual artist, how would I paint it? If I were a film maker, what would my film be about? This technique of distantiation was far harder to use than I anticipated, with each piece revealing the extent to which one can be unconsciously imbricated in hegemonic practices and discursive régimes, even whilst attempting to write 'against the grain' of what you already know. Fictionalising the research in this way also provided a site a little removed from the world of lived experience, which permitted exploration of various practical and moral dilemmas related to disability, difference, equity, inclusion and methodologically allowed the possibility to reassert the significance of memory, affect and imagination to pedagogy. These pieces, in turn, provided opportunities for audiences of critical friends to experience and interrogate the work in a way that was intrapersonal (Lomax, 1999), embedded and contextualised in our professional practices and working lives. Perhaps what was most significant in terms of the psychological process of coming to understand who one is as a teacher, was that they also offered a form of protest against any totalising, monotheic view of what constitutes teacher or learner, suggesting instead various intimations of teacher as 'cumulative cultural text' (Weber and Mitchell, 1995).

In *The Discipline and Practice of Qualitative Research*, Denzin and Lincoln (2000:3-5) describe how qualitative researchers are now using

> ...personal experience; introspection; life story; interview; artefacts; cultural texts and productions; observational, historical, interactional, and visual texts – that describe routine and problematic moments and meanings in individuals' lives. Accordingly, qualitative researchers deploy a wide variety of interconnected interpretive practices, hoping always to get a better understanding of the subject matter in hand... The qualitative researcher may take on multiple and gendered images: scientist, naturalist, fieldworker, journalist, social critic artist, performer, jazz musician, filmmaker, quilt maker, essayist. The many methodological practices of qualitative research may be viewed as soft science, journalism, ethnography, bricolage, quilt making or montage.

And

> In texts based on metaphors of montage, quilt making and jazz improvisation, many different things are going on at the same time – different voices, different perspectives, points of views, angles of vision. Like performance texts, works that use montage simultaneously create and enact moral meaning. They move from the personal to the political, the local to the historical and the cultural. These are dialogic texts. They presume an active audience. They create spaces for give-and-take between reader and writer.

The Dramatic Turn

My doctoral thesis (Perselli, 2001a) refers to the occasions where I presented my fictional pieces for critical review as a Social Stage and, following the theatre director Peter Brook (1968), the creative endeavour as the Empty Space. I think that the possibilities of locating my personal identity as a SENCO (historically, sociologically, politically), then distancing myself from this persona, becoming the imaginary Other: artist, poet, storyteller, filmmaker, artist again, added perspectival dimensions which eventually facilitated new ways of being in the classroom. I came to realise that whilst control of teaching and learning in England may appear to have been ceded to centralist forces, the contexts in which schooling takes place, diverse, highly unpredictable and therefore unstable, cannot possibly assume homogeneous groups of teachers or learners for whom a 'done-to' metanarrative or model of education will work. Without wishing to fetishise Difference, the fictional writing revealed to me not only the problematical role of the SENCO role but also my own imbrication in a western, liberal, individualist society and culture, which I must now understand as irrelevant (if not alien) to many of the adults and children with whom I work. I would also add that this explicit understanding of the deep relevance of my culture to my practice as a teacher educator has helped me feel great respect for the significance of culture in general, and the cultures of others specifically, wherever and whenever education is taking place.

Representation and Voice

Accepting Patti Lather's view that research is 'a way of being at risk' (Lather, 1991; Stronach and MacLure, 1997), performance media can offer helpful means towards exploration of the indeterminate and unstable nature of education as personal, social and political dis/ engagement. Surrealism, the interpretation of dreams and the uses of metaphor and allegory (Perselli, 2001b; 2001c) are particular tools of critical creativity which interested me when representing and synthesising my research data. For the audiences who participated in the interrogation and critique of my work, viewing this as performance facilitated political questions of the kind: Who has permission to speak? In whose interest? What else is happening here? What is missing? This raised issues of identity and agency which are pertinent to the ethical and political responsibilities of the researcher in general (Gitlin, 1994) and within the highly significant fields of inclusion and specifically special educational needs (Barnes and Mercer, 1997; Clough and Barton, 1998).

My research was linguistically orientated in so far as I recognised a necessity to separate Special from Needs, Curriculum from National and Technical from Rational. It was necessary to reconfigure my practice along different lines to these seemingly mandatory positions in a system where teachers were being told what to think and do, rather than thinking and acting in response to what we can learn, through our academic and local communities, from the world of lived experience around us. To summarise: I used first poetry: *Exposition, A Birthday Ode, A Magic Box, Giocco delle Parti, Silver and Gold,* then story and drama: *A Magic Box, Two Teaching Experiences, Gemma in a Blue Dress, The Boyzone,* to describe my teaching interventions with pupils. Each of these was shared (accompanied by explanatory supporting material) with the various learning communities that became accessible to me at the time: practitioners in the field of infant education and special educational needs, my doctoral research group, audiences at academic conferences. Each critical commentary fed into the subsequent piece of writing, enabling me to revisit the data reflexively through a variety of social and literary lenses: dis/ability, race, gender and sexuality and social class. Whilst suitably sceptical in their responses to these representations in terms of the rightness of what was said or done, colleagues reacted favourably to the method: 'As someone who has never... who doesn't know how to represent my practice, I found the stories very helpful'; 'It was your learning journey you were sharing with us' (*The SENCO Support Group*).

The Visual Turn

Method and practice gradually informed one another, becoming enfolded or 'wrapped around' each other (Stronach and MacLure, 1997), as the visual imagery evoked through story telling gave way to concrete visual media such as photography, painting and drawing in the classroom. I began to really appreciate the significance of the visual (Perselli, 1999a, 1999b, 1999c), by providing extended opportunities to draw or paint for pupils in the (self-designated) Boyzone (metamorphosed as *Six Nomadic Scholars*, below); through camera work to record learning progress and enhance the sense of self-in-space and self-in-community for my pupils with Down syndrome (portrayed in company as *Adnan, Gemma, James and Fee*) and through photographic displays strategically positioned around the school. These activities enlarged the scope of my political and emotional engagement in my work, whilst enriching the experiences of the children.

I hasten to add that these individual aspects of praxis were by no means especially innovative, but they were problematic. They were deliberate, politically and ideologically motivated acts that did not always bear up to the scrutiny of keen eyes and ears (Prosser, 1998: 97-112; Mitchell and Weber, 1999: 1-9), with many foreseen and un-foreseen issues of identity and representation, of ethics and politics emerging. However, the act of writing the stories, creating visual arte-facts, presenting these to a wide variety of audiences, and revisiting and synthesising the data facilitated a new and different take on prac-tice that worked both with and against the *status quo*. The dis-ciplinary boundary crossing (Rowland, 2003), if not the collapse of boundary divisions in SEN, had begun.

Visual media, in particular, were means towards reaching audiences who were not formally engaged in the research. It was often the sur-prise reactions of others, such as my school-based colleague's response to a wall display to celebrate the work of teachers and learning sup-port assistants, created for the opening of a new school building: 'So why are there no men in it?' (see also Colley *ibid.*) which provoked tangential thought and jolted the research into new territory. In parti-cular there were my own mis/understandings around dis/ability and my inability to confront what Deborah Britzman powerfully arti-culates as 'difficult knowledge' (Britzman, 1998). I returned to this frequently and especially in the allegorical *Do you like my picture, Dad?* (printed below), where it has become inextricably linked with other difficult knowledges such as patriarchy and parental pride.

The Dramatic Turn

Finally then, I have included here the Duologue *A Personal Preview*, which I wrote and performed at the end of the project, just before the *viva voce* examination of the thesis (*An Assessment Exercise*, printed below). There are two characters in this dramatisation: the Curator; a gallery attendant in a small German town (which had connections and disconnections with mainland Europe, nostalgically construed, and a theme in the thesis, e.g. *Foucault's Flat*), where the art work of a minor artist, 'Perselli', is on display; and an unidentified male visitor to the show, with whom she engages in conversation about the ex-hibits. Each of these pieces refers to an aspect of the research which took place at an earlier stage, now symbolically and objectively transformed. The writing here acts as both a projection forward during that long, final writing-up period when other audiences are suddenly unavailable, and a reflective glance backwards, which surprisingly, also provided a sense of closure on the events and persons whom 'we love and let go' (*Demeter as Teacher, her seeds spilling from her box*).

A Personal Preview is an autobiography in allegorical, miniature form, in which a teacher of special educational needs reviews her life-world, conjuring it as a series of art works with questions and critical commentary. A final resistance has been to explain it in concrete terms, but without destroying its deliberate tendency towards postmodern ambiguity. Conversations with the editors of this book have yielded detailed discussion about how to offer something so contextually embedded, without running the risk of accusations of deliberate obfuscation for the reader; a point frequently raised by critics of work in the postmodern. Personally I do not see this as a postmodern text, although I like Stronach and MacLure's (1997) metaphor of a map best read folded, so that intimate details are less significant than distantiation; taking the long view over time and space as well as culture. I therefore suggest viewing the images presented here like a folded map, knowing they are missing something, but also knowing that they may also not recognise it if they see it.

Autobiographical writing within the bounded context of a self-study research is problematic (as shown in the role of the SENCO), a finite representation (a doctoral thesis) leaves much that is unsaid, and its self-disclosures can conceal at least as much as it reveals. One shocking revelation which came to me almost too late was that in my enthusiasm for artistic dis/guises and distantiation I had forgotten that I started out as a practising classical musician. I brought this additional dimension to my SENCO persona which, I now suspect with no little irony, actually meant the most to the children I worked with. So there were secret skills, influences and even an erasure of the self in my thesis which the Preview rather hastily and inadequately recovers, explained only via a handful of acknowledgements in the bibliography. This sense of self-negation may well be unfamiliar to readers working in a less harsh environment, or who perceive their circumstances differently, but to those among us who might or might not describe themselves as postmodernists, for whom gaps and slippages of one kind or another constitute the actual/other story of a life, there could be some resonances. Regarding validation or evaluation, for readers in comparable contexts and settings, a guiding question might be: 'This was how I saw it at the time; how was it for you?' For those to whom the writing is unfamiliar or strange, a methodological alternative might be: 'If this was your Personal Preview (or indeed, collaborative endeavour), what would you put there?'

Duologue: A Personal Preview

Curator: ... Well during the late 70s and early 80s Perselli had been working on these huge canvasses, which she called her 'Curricula'. Many of them, as you may have noticed, are unsigned, and often it is not clear which were done by the maestra and which by apprentices; its simply wasn't considered important. However, by the 1990s these can be seen to be out of step with the times. The 1990s was a period of immense richness and variety, but also of factions. There were the Conceptualists, the Technicists, the Lyricists; some of whom never actually talked to each other. This was also a time of suspicion and censorship; accusations were flying about painters who couldn't paint, learners who couldn't learn, teachers who couldn't teach, *und so weiter*. For many different reasons the viewing public wanted names, dates and preferably faces; work produced through collaboration, especially if it offered no external verification, was considered suspect or 'inauthentic'.

So Perselli began to concentrate her attention on intimate portraits from her personal life, drawn primarily from experience and memory. Some of these you will have seen before; for example the ones we have grouped under 'Life Stages':

> Kids on Shipley Bridge (1968)
> Jacqueline Du Pré
> Emma Kirkby
> Sylvia Plath (Bread, Milk, Sheep in Fog)

> Two Neighbours
> The SENCO Support Group (Pathological Carers!)
> Demeter as Teacher, her Seeds Spilling from her Box
> Mrs. Turner cutting the grass (who chose not to reveal the secrets of her youth)

and

> Maxine Greene.

Here we have also the installation,

My Desk

which is quite well known.

Visitor: Perselli was only interested in painting women?

Curator: No, Not at all! Over time the artist became curious about particular themes of human experience: hegemony and passion, patriarchy and vulnerability, explored across the genders and genres; for example in the Cartoons:

Three Hunky Dorys (Bigbury-on-Sea, 2000)
Crazy Naked Hitchhiker (he collects useless correlations)
Anal Musings
High Windows
The Pied Piper (David Munroe, British Broadcasting
Corporation, 1972)

and

Rach. 3

a study of an early boyfriend.

The themes become more overtly reflexive in the paintings of children:

Aubrey and Paul
Brown Class (1996)
Adnan, Gemma, James and Fee

and in these charcoal drawings of an unusual young lad:

J. Lewis Borges.

If you go outside you will find sculptures of a group of small boys, inspired by the First Nations art of North America; 'Sometimes we take something which was made by the Other and turn it into something else':

Six Nomadic Scholars

And then of course there is

Foucault's Flat (this Body, this Paper, this Fire)

and

Man Asleep, Radio On.

Perselli was uncomfortable, if unapologetic, regarding the female gaze. In fact there is a political message in the emotionality of this last picture which is easy to miss in the more obvious drama of the composition.

Perhaps the political commentary comes out more strongly in

Watcher Watched O'er

a figure in a curious kind of mask; 'bloodless, sexless and voided'

and very explicitly in

An Assessment Exercise

which is a more formal, realist composition. Here we have a group of serious-minded people examining documents at a large board-room type table. 'It's not just that everything is dangerous; everything is publicable'. The pottery in the niches is from the late nineteen sixties, by the way. It's by Marian de Trey.

Visitor: So tell me about this space here.

Curator: A yes,

A Bad Hair Day.

This picture was withdrawn at the artist's request. It was considered obscene under the 'Advice and Guidelines on Approved Obscenities for Non-Commissioned Artists Remaining in Residence, Fourth Revision'.

Visitor: And was it?

Curator: Obscene? O yes! But it also poked fun at government, which of course was strictly forbidden. For that one you would need to go to the Archive.

Visitor: And this next painting is a self-portrait, I believe?

Curator: Here we see two female figures; a little girl standing on a table, drawing on a vast whiteboard...

Visitor: She is gorgeous; a beautiful Infanta!

Curator: ... and a woman on her haunches, in the low right-hand side of the frame, offering her some coloured pens. The room is clearly a classroom, although there are various objects in the fore-ground which seem not to belong: a slice of chocolate cake on a porcelain plate; hearing aids thrown in the waste basket. There is tinsel and wrapping paper, toy cars, hair ornaments – perhaps it is the child's birthday. However the placing of the objects suggests a symbolical significance also.

The position of the woman is interesting, we feel we know this gesture; the sense of alertness and restraint in the torso reminiscent maybe of the prompter at the side of the stage, or the parent behind the finishing line at a children's sports day; anxious and exhilarated at the same moment.

One wall of the classroom is made of glass. Outside we see a man hurrying by. He seems to have caught the eye of someone, but it isn't the child or the woman. Indeed, if you look carefully you will notice a small circle of light bouncing off the whiteboard; someone else, outside the frame, is taking a photograph.

Visitor: The photograph used for the portrait?

Curator: Well it could have been; but actually the flash from the camera serves as a device to reconcile a specific technical problem. It's as though the artist deliberately made things difficult for herself by painting the child in front of this huge whiteboard. If you think about it, it's a strange backdrop for such an ostensibly classical portrait. If there were a photograph, it would be disastrous in terms of light distribution. What the camera does, out of frame, is refract the glare, bounce it away from the figures; a technical problem is resolved by technical means.

Visitor: And the tiny design the girl is making on the whiteboard – haven't we seen that somewhere before?

Curator: The child's drawing? Yes! Here it appears as a postcard-sized version of a detail of the large mural you will have encountered in the entrance.

Visitor: Perselli was trying to paint like a child?

Curator: No. Ha! For the curators the mural is amusing because many people think the figures in it have some kind of 'postmodern' significances. But Perselli didn't actually paint the mural. If you go back and look at it again you will recognise particular images: The Witch, The Pirates, The Shark, The Chequered Flag, The Boy Running, The Sun, The Face, The Trees in the Good Snow, An Electrical Circuit, A Party Frock. Each section was done by a child and if you look along the bottom of the canvass you will see their tentative attempts at painting their names. In this instance, who made the pictures – and where the artists are coming from – is at least as significant as what the images 'mean'. So in that sense I suppose you could argue that the mural is 'postmodern'.

Visitor: And this self-portrait of the woman and the girl – the title is?

Curator: .

Do you like my picture, Dad?

It's a question casually thrown out, which begs other questions. Does the man outside the glass hear her? What is he going to do? Will he nod politely to the photographer and hurry on? He is late for something – Parents' Evening perhaps? A meeting with his daughter's teachers? But if this is a school, Where are the others? Why are there three adults to one child; each in their separate force field? The ingenuous cunning of the child's question catches up familiar themes: patriarchy, vulnerability, the gesture apprehended, things thrown into suspension. Some essence of the artist's experience lies in this picture, I think – although I am not sure she would have put it that way.

Visitor: I see. And... in terms of subsequent works...?

Curator: A series of acrylics:

18 Euphoric Studies of Animal Lovers

in homage to Hockney; but they're out on loan. In America I believe.

Visitor: Sounds interesting.

Curator: There are some things there I feel sure you would enjoy [smiles].

Visitor: Yes! But in any case I... I really must be going now. You are leaving also?

Curator: Not just yet; the gallery stays open late on Tuesdays.

Visitor: Oh well, good night then, and... thank you! Vielen Dank!

Curator: It's been my pleasure.

References

Barnes, C and Mercer, G (eds) (1997) *Doing Disability Research*. Leeds: The Disability Press

Britzman, D P (1998) *Lost Subjects, Contested Objects: Towards a psychoanalytic inquiry of learning*. Albany: State University of New York Press

Brook, P (1968) *The Empty Space*. Harmondsworth: Penguin

Bullough, R V and Pinnegar, S (2001) Guidelines for quality in autobiographical forms, in: *Educational Researcher*, 30(3): 13-23

Clough, P and Barton, L (eds) (1998) *Articulating with Difficulty: Research voices in inclusive education*. London: Paul Chapman

Cole, A and McIntyre, M (1998) Reflections on 'Dance Me to an Understanding of Teaching', Conversations in Community: Proceedings of the Second International Conference of the Self-Study of Teacher Education Practice. Herstmoneux: S-STEP

Colley, H (2003) The myth of mentor as a double régime of truth: producing docility and devotion in engagement mentoring with 'disaffected' youth, in: Satterthwaite, J, Atkinson, E and Gale, E (eds) *Discourse, Power, Resistance: Challenging the rhetoric of contemporary education*. Stoke on Trent: Trentham Books

Denzin, N K and Lincoln, Y S (eds) (2000) *Handbook of Qualitative Research* (2nd ed). Thousand Oaks: Sage

Gazetas, A (2000) *Imagining Selves: The politics of representation, film narratives and adult education*. New York: Peter Lang

Giroux, H (1992) *Border Crossings: Cultural workers and the politics of education*. New York and London: Routledge

Gitlin, A (1994) (ed) *Power and Method: Political activism and educational research*. New York and London: Routledge

Hamilton, M L, Pinnegar, S, Russell, T, Loughran, J and LaBoskey, V (eds) (1998) *Reconceptualising Teaching Practice: Self-study in teacher education*. London and Philadelphia: Falmer

Lather, P (1991) *Getting Smart: Feminist research and pedagogy with/in the postmodern*. New York and London: Routledge

Lomax, P (1999) Working together for educative community through research. Presidential Address to the British Educational Research Association Annual Conference, The Queen's University, Belfast, 1999, in: *British Educational Research Journal*, 25(1): 5-22

Mitchell, C and Weber, S (1999) *Reinventing Ourselves as Teachers: Beyond Nostalgia*. London and Philadelphia: Falmer

Perselli, V (1999a) Representing Rory: with my heart and my head. An action researcher's investigation into inclusive education for pupils with learning difficulties. Paper presented at the Annual Conference of the American Educational Research Association, Montreal, April

Perselli, V (1999b) 'All the way to America': explaining some significances of multiple forms of representation in the work of a child with Down syndrome. Paper presented at the 6th Annual International Conference on Teacher Research, Magog, Eastern Townships, Quebec, April

Perselli, V (1999c) Demonstrating progression in the work of my pupil via visual records. Paper presented at the Annual Conference of the British Educational Research Association, University of Sussex, Brighton, September

Perselli V (2001a) The Importance of Being... an Artist: Interpreting the challenge of inclusion in infant mainstream education; a self-study, action research approach. Unpublished PhD Thesis, Kingston University, UK

Perselli, V (2001b) Two experiences of teaching being: the feminine imaginary in education research. Paper presented at the 8th Annual International Conference on Teacher Research, Vancouver, April

Perselli, V (2001c) Two experiences of teaching being: film as fiction in education research. Paper presented at the Annual Conference of the British Educational Research Association, University of Leeds, September

Perselli, V (2004a forthcoming) Re-imagining research, re-presenting the self: putting arts media to work in the analysis and synthesis of data on 'difference' and '(dis)ability', in: *International Journal of Qualitative Studies in Education*, forthcoming

Perselli, V (2004b forthcoming) Teaching for England: five poems, in: *Cultural Studies, Critical Methodologies* (forthcoming)

Perselli, V (2004c forthcoming) Heavy fuel, in: O'Reilly Scanlon, K, Weber, S and Mitchell, C (eds) *Just who do we think we are? Methodologies for self-study in teacher education*. London and Philadelphia: Falmer

Prosser, J (1998) (ed.) *Image-based Research: A sourcebook for qualitative researchers*. London and Philadelphia: Falmer

Rowland, S (2003) Learning to comply, learning to contest, in: Satterthwaite, J, Atkinson, E and Gale, K (eds) *Discourse, Power, Resistance: Challenging the rhetoric of contemporary education*. Stoke on Trent: Trentham Books

Schratz, M (2001) A visual approach to evaluation in schools. Paper presented at the Second Annual Conference of the Centre for Applied Research in Education, University of East Anglia, July

Stronach, I and MacLure, M (1997) *Educational Research Undone: The postmodern embrace*. Buckingham: Open University Press

Walker, R (2001) Ways of using pictures (in social research). Paper presented to the Second Annual Conference of the Centre for Applied Research in Education, University of East Anglia, July

Weber, S and Mitchell, C (1995) *'That's funny, you don't look like a teacher': Interrogating Images and Identity in Popular Culture*. London and Philadelphia: Falmer

Winter, R, Buck, A and Sobiechowska, P (1999) *Professional Experience and the Investigative Imagination: The art of reflective writing*. London and New York: Routledge

Additional sources of inspiration include:

Margaret Atwood (1989) *Cat's Eye*. London: Bloomsbury

Jorge Luis Borges (Tr Hurley, A) (1998) *Fictions* (1941-44). Harmondsworth: Penguin

Maxine Greene (2000) In search of metaphor: a fireside chat with Maxine Greene. Featured Session, Annual Meeting of the American Educational Research Association, New Orleans, April

Philip Larkin (1974) *High Windows*. London: Faber and Faber

Sylvia Plath (1965) *Ariel*. London: Faber and Faber

Carol Shields (1984) Mrs. Turner Cutting the Grass, in: *Various Miracles*. Harmondsworth: Penguin

Sergei Rachmaninov *Piano Concerto No. 3*

The early performances and recorded works of Emma Kirkby

The recorded works of David Munroe

Contributors

Michael W. Apple is the John Bascom Professor of Curriculum and Instruction and Educational Policy Studies at the University of Wisconsin, Madison. He has written extensively on the relationship between culture and power in education. Among his recent books are *Official Knowledge, Educating The 'Right' Way: Markets, Standards, God, And Inequality, And The State And The Politics Of Knowledge*. His book *Ideology And Curriculum* has been selected as one of the most important books in education in the 20th Century and a 25th Anniversary Third Edition will be published in the Spring of 2004.

Elizabeth Atkinson is a Reader in Social and Educational Inquiry in the School of Education and Lifelong Learning at Sunderland University, UK. Her research and writing bring postmodern perspectives to bear on issues of identity, policy and practice in the educational arena.

Alan Bleakley is a Senior Research Fellow, Peninsula Medical School, Universities of Exeter and Plymouth. He is a medical educator, researching and stimulating through collaborative inquiry a variety of multi-professional clinical change practices including more effective team work in operating theatres. He is also involved in implementing a core Medical Humanities Undergraduate and postgraduate curriculum. He is widely published in Medical Education, Education and Psychology. His last book *The Animalising Imagination* is published by Macmillan (2000).

Richard Bond is Director of the Centre for Adult Studies and Distance Learning, Brock University, Canada. He has long been fascinated by cultural diversity and intra-cultural similarities. He teaches Politics of Education and Organsational Behaviours in Educational Institutions in the graduate department of the Faculty of Education. He is currently considering a project in which the adult education programme he supervises can be adapted to accommodate the culture of Québec and the language of French Canada.

Mike Cole is Senior Lecturer in Education at the University of Brighton. Recent publications include *Red Chalk: On Schooling, Capitalism and Politics*, Brighton: Institute for Education Policy Studies (2001); *Schooling and Equality: Fact Concept and Policy*, London: Kogan Page (2001); *Education Equality and Human Rights*, London: Routledge/Falmer (2002); *Marxism Against Postmodernism in Educational Theory*, Lanham, MD: Lexington Press (2002) and *Professional Values and Practice for Teachers and Student Teachers*, London: David Fulton (2003). He is the author of *Marxism, Postmodernism And Education: Pasts, Presents And Futures*, London: Routledge/Falmer (forthcoming, 2005).

John Danvers is Teaching Fellow and MA Programme Director (Art and Design), University of Plymouth. His research interests include: philosophies of art practice (particularly Buddhism and pragmatism); experimental texts and postmodern poetics; and developing a radical pedagogy for art. He is currently working on a book entitled *Picturing Mind*. As an art practitioner he has exhibited in Europe, North America, Australia and UK, and is currently engaged in producing a multi-narrative work for the internet.
Website: www.johndanversart.co.uk
Email: j.danvers@plymouth.ac.uk

Jean McNiff is an independent researcher, living in Dorset and working in international contexts. She is Adjunct Professor at the University of Limerick, and a Visiting Fellow at the University of the West of England. She writes extensively about the power of professional learning for the sustainability of social orders that are animated by a spirit of freedom, fairness, love and beauty for all. You can reach her at http://www.jeanmcniff.com

Farid Panjwani is a Senior Instructor at the Institute for the Study of Muslim Civilisations, Aga Khan University, London. He has a range of teaching, training and work experience in the fields of Islamic Studies, Education and Management. Before starting at his current position, Farid was extensively involved in the design of an international curriculum on the cultures, history and faith of Muslim people. He is currently undertaking doctoral studies in Philosophy of Education at the University of Oxford.

Victoria Perselli is a senior lecturer in education at Kingston University, UK, where she teachers courses in qualitative research methods, special educational needs and inclusive education. Her prior work includes a 5-year self-study investigating the role of the coordinator for Special Educational Needs in mainstream education. Her current interests include the rereading of European high theory, also the use of narrative and Performance Arts Media as forms of representation and interpretation in qualitative research.

Halleli Pinson is a research associate at the Faculty of Education, University of Cambridge. She is currently engaged with a new research project on the schooling experiences of asylum seeking adolescents in the UK. She has recently completed her PhD in Cambridge University, which explored the discursive formation of political identities among Jewish and Palestinian Israeli youth and the ways in which Citizenship Education acts as a space in which meanings and identities are negotiated.

Jerome Satterthwaite teaches in the Faculty of Education at the University of Plymouth. He is the organiser of the Plymouth conferences on Discourse, Power, Resistance which are held in April each year.

Terry Wrigley teaches at the University of Edinburgh. He edits the journal *Improving Schools*. His first book *The Power to Learn* (2000), a study of highly successful inner city schools with large numbers of Asian pupils, illustrates how empowerment rather than increasing surveillance is the key to their success. *Schools of Hope* (2003) challenges the dominant model of School Improvement and calls for a new focus on democracy, global citizenship and social justice.

Index

205